NEW PRODUCT LAUNCH

10 PROVEN STRATEGIES

New Product Launch

10 PROVEN STRATEGIES

JOAN SCHNEIDER

WITH JEANNE YOCUM

STAGNITO COMMUNICATIONS, INC.

AN MWC COMPANY

DEERFIELD, ILLINOIS

Printed in the United States of America

Published in 2004 by Stagnito Communications Inc., Deerfield, Illinois 60015

New Product Launch: 10 Proven Strategies
Schneider, Joan

Includes notes and index

ISBN 0-9752979-0-2

Photos reprinted with permission

Cover Design and Jacket: Michael J. Escobedo
Book Design and Layout: Richard M. Chung

*To celebrate Rose Norden,
my grandmother, whose indomitable
spirit guides me to never give up,
no matter what the obstacle.*

— Joan Schneider

*In loving memory of my father,
J. Arthur Yocum, who taught me
to believe in myself.*

— Jeanne Yocum

Mission:

The mission of this book is to motivate consumer products companies and their marketing partners to thoroughly rethink their approach to the critical launch phase of new product development. Our goal is to help companies beat the high new product failure rate by creating more innovative, effective launch campaigns.

CONTENTS

SECTION 7

GETTING IT DONE: LAUNCH TOOLS & TECHNIQUES

F **or more than 35 years,** I have listened to every conceivable reason why new product introductions in the food, beverage, packaging, and non-foods markets have failed at a rate of 75 percent. Careers and reputations have been built and diminished by the success or failure of new products placed in the marketplace. Billions of dollars have been wasted in the search for the Holy Grail of the "Big Hit." And yet the beat goes on as companies strive to create the magic formula that will strike the mother lode of new product success — at a rate of 33,000 new product, introductions annually, according to Productscan Online.

I have talked to hundreds of retailers, manufacturers and suppliers over the years about how to improve the number of new product successes, and found myself focusing on the negative approach to achieving profitability and riches. For example, I've preached about the travails of poor idea generation; how changing consumer demographics are misunderstood; the conflict within multifunctional (or perhaps largely dysfunctional) product teams; launching products too quickly; poor positioning, and the lack of management support. And of course, there's waiting until the new product is nearly ready to be shipped before starting to plan the launch. Although I've put a lot of thought into the poor new product success rate — and have exchanged ideas and experiences with exceptional thinkers on the subject — I could not advise, with certainty, the most appropriate course of action to guarantee positive results.

Because new products are the lifeblood of growth for consumer goods companies, I decided to do something about the subject. Stagnito Communications launched its own new product in 2001 called *Stagnito's New Products Magazine*. Its purpose: to improve the success of new product launches. The magazine has turned out to be a winner, both in critical acclaim as well as in growth. And because of this new magazine, I met Joan Schneider.

Joan, founder and president of Schneider & Associates, who contacted me in 2002 to present a groundbreaking research study titled The Schneider/Boston University New Products Launch Report, a joint academic and field project examining how marketers launch new products. Joan followed up her original research with the Harris Interactive/Schneider 2002 Most Memorable New Products Survey, looking at new product launches and why consumers found them memorable. I was extremely impressed with the research, and followed up with a meeting to discuss a co-ventured new products research project. Joan surprised me in May 2003 with the proposal to write a book devoted to new product launches, and asked SCI to publish it.

Like any good publisher, I made it difficult for Joan to sell her idea to me. But her professionalism in developing the book outline, sample chapters, promotional program and especially the point-of-difference premise made the decision an easy one. Everything was summarized by this thesis: Joan Schneider decided to investigate how to improve the number of new product successes. The overwhelming conclusion: The launch stage of the new product process determines the difference between a winner and loser.

Joan, with co-author Jeanne Yocum, began writing *New Product Launch: 10 Proven Strategies*. The book covers critically important issues seldom reported in detail. Issues such as the evolution of parallel product development to cross-functional new product teams; the benefits or demerits of test marketing and market research; the controversial elements of slotting allowances and failure fees; price/value relationships; alternative methods of distribution; and in-depth case histories. While there have been volumes written about the new products process, there has been little written about the actual launch process in this manner.

A special side benefit of this relationship has been the compilation of some trend-focused, ground-breaking research. This year we published the Schneider/Stagnito Communications 2003 Most Memorable New Products Survey. The information gathered from these unique studies is included in the book.

So, for the first time in many years, I believe that new products might actually see their number of victories increase. *New Product Launch* provides a roadmap to guide new products from launch to success in a time-tested, positive manner. If you're a CEO, brand or marketing manager, advertising or public relations executive, or a member of a multi-functional team, I promise you will approach your next new product launch with a new attitude.

I know I will.

Harry Stagnito
President & CEO
Stagnito Communications, Inc.

----------------- **ACKNOWLEDGMENTS** -----------------

Acknowledgments from Joan Schneider

A**s a first-time author,** I have so many people to thank for cheering me on. This book might never have happened without my Harvard Business School buddies Anne Jardine, whose idea it was to pursue launch as a differentiator for Schneider & Associates, and Marti Smye, Ph.D., who made me promise I would write a book about launch. I agreed to consider the idea as I set off for Key West on a motorcycle trip with my husband, Ron Egalka. Ron not only encouraged me to start the book, but made it possible for me to finish it by hooking me up via cellular modem so I could work anywhere (which turned out to be everywhere, including on our vacations). His belief in my abilities and his love are what kept me going, day after day.

A special thanks to Professor Ben Shapiro of Harvard Business School, who told me that launch was an underinvestigated area of new product development and introduced me to Professor Susan Fournier, Ph.D., who helped me research and develop the concepts that were the basis for our first study, the Schneider/Boston University New Product Launch Report.

Without Dr. Michael Elasmer and Kumiko Aoki of Boston University's Communication Research Center, we'd never have completed the research with the 100 brand and product managers that provided the basis for this book. With encouragement from my staff, Jennifer Bonner, Anthony Ramos, and Julie Hall, we've continued to research the topic of launch with two additional studies, the Most Memorable New Product Launch surveys of 2002 and 2003. With their help and continued support, I was able to write the book and keep Schneider & Associates running smoothly. My heartfelt thanks go to Jeanne Yocum, my coauthor, with whom I've had the privilege of working for the past 20 years. Not only are we friends, but we have the ability to keep up with our deadlines and still have a few laughs along the way.

Last but not least, I'd like to thank my mom and dad, Marilyn and Len Schneider, for their unwavering encouragement for everything I do. I am grateful for their enthusiasm, optimism, and zeal for life, which contributed the DNA that drives me to succeed, no matter what the obstacles.

Acknowledgments from Jeanne Yocum

Thanks to all those strangers who responded to my ProfNet queries and took time out of busy schedules for phone interviews. Many of you made it into the book, but some insights ended up on the cutting room floor due to space constraints; for that, I apologize and hope it won't keep you from taking my phone call the next time!

Joan Schneider continues to be an excellent writing partner and an even better friend. Writing a book together is an extreme test for any relationship. Fortunately, Joan and I met the challenge — mostly, I believe, because of the strong affection and respect we have for each other. We're even talking about our *next* book already! Thanks for inviting me along for the ride, dear friend.

Joint Thanks

Thanks to our agent, Al Zuckerman of Writer's House, who not only found our idea to be "interesting," but had the foresight to persuade Harry Stagnito, president of Stagnito Communications, to publish this book as the first in its new publishing division. Our heartfelt thanks go to Joan Holleran and Pierce Hollingsworth, our coaches at Stagnito, who provided us with a great editor, Elizabeth

"Lib" Brewster, who made our prose tighter and more concise. Thanks, too, to the creative force of cover designer Michael Escobedo, whose work likely lured you to this book in the first place, and graphic designer Richard Chung, who made the book look its best.

We would also like to thank our talented research team, composed of Meredith Veysey, Liz Slavkovsky, and Joni Fraser, for their dedication and contributions to *New Product Launch: 10 Proven Strategies.*

Finally, this book would not have been possible without the contributions of the many individuals whose insight and enthusiasm were instrumental throughout the entire process, from inception to final editing. We truly appreciate those CEOs and marketing executives who took the time to be interviewed and who lent their names and stories to illuminate the concepts set forth in these pages.

We extend special thanks to:

Domenic Antonellis of NECCO, Lara Bandler and Rohan Oza of Energy Brands Inc., Cori Barrett of Access Communications, Jennifer Barrett of Newsweek.msnbc.com, Eric Baty, formerly of Consolidated Sales Network and now COO of Café Bom Dia, Pete Blackshaw of Intelliseek, Jonathan Bloom of McGrath/Power PR, Tom Bradley of Mintz & Hoke, Sal Cataldi of Cataldi PR, Carol Cone of Cone, Inc., Jennifer Cue of Jones Soda Company, Joel Curran and Marty Ellery of CKPR, Skip Dampier of Ross Creative + Strategy, Marilyn Darling of Signet Consulting Group, Chris Donnelly of GeigerDonnelly Marketing LLC, Rich Doucette of Alloy Marketing and Promotions, Carey Earle of Harvest Communications, Kim Feil of Mosaic InfoForce LLP, Marcy Freeman of Colgate Palmolive Company, author and marketing guru Seth Godin, Joe Grimaldi of Mullen Advertising Inc., Justin Holloway of Hill, Holliday, Connors, Cosmopulos Inc., Shel Hurwtiz of FrugalMarketing.com, Ted Jursek of Naive Wisdom, PSF, Eric Kraus of The Gillette Company, Steve Linstrom and John Nabholz of The Schwan Food Company, Jean Lizotte of Old Mother Hubbard, Rebecca Maddox of Maddox Smye LLC, Marina Maher of Marina Maher Communications, Walter Mills of PARTNERS+simons, Hector Marinez and Kevin Winston of Porter Novelli Bay Area, Tom Merrick and Scott Russell of MRA Group, Sheryl O'Loughlin and Dean Mayer of Clif Bar Inc., Jeff Pacione of

Catapult Thinking, John Parham of Parham Santana, Ellen Ratchye-Foster of Burning Glass Consulting, John Rattigan of Colorado Boxed Beef Company, Al Ries of Ries & Ries, John Rocke of RMH Foods, Todd Seisser of Saatchi & Saatchi, Michael Silverstein of Boston Consulting Group, Valerie Skala of Information Resources, Inc., Samantha Skey and Jodi Smith of 360 Youth, Pete Slosberg of Cocoa Pete's Chocolate Adventures, Mark Snieder of AcuPOLL, Mike Swenson of Barkley Evergreen & Partners, Inc., Alan Taylor of Alan Taylor Communications, John Vecchione of Dermaläge, Tim Volk of Kelliher Samets Volk, and Fannie Young of Schiefflin & Somerset.

NEW PRODUCT LAUNCH

10 PROVEN STRATEGIES

INTRODUCTION

THE LAUNCH FRENZY

Yesterday, **92 new products** in the food, beverage, health and beauty aids, household, and pet product categories were introduced to American consumers. Today, 92 more new products will be launched, and tomorrow 92 more new products will hit store shelves. And so on and so on for all 365 days of the year.

Do the math, and you'll find that consumers are confronted with more than 33,000 new products annually in these categories — and this has been happening since 2000[1]. That figure, amazing as it is, doesn't include consumer electronics, cars, housewares, toys, fashions, books, CDs, movies, or the consumer-oriented services that are introduced each year.

And you were wondering why it's so hard to get a little attention for your company's latest consumer gizmo or taste treat?

Even in the go-go 1990s, the pace of new product introductions wasn't nearly this crazed. In 1992, for instance, only 15,886 new products were released in the food, beverage, health and beauty aids, pet, and household categories. Throughout the decade, that figure gradually moved up by several thousand each year to reach 25,928 in 1999.

But in 2000, all hell broke loose, and the figure jumped by over 6,000, reaching 31,432. In 2001, the number was up again, with

32,025 new packaged goods products being released. When the recession hit, new product launches decreased slightly, to 31,785 in 2002. In 2003, though, another new record was established with 33,678 new products debuting in the packaged goods arena, up 6 percent from just the previous year.

What's going on here?

Welcome to the new product launch frenzy of the 21st century. In the battle for consumer attention, profits, and market share, corporate America has fully embraced the notion that newer is better. Whether unveiling a breakthrough technology or a simple line extension, companies of all types and sizes want to be able to shout from the rooftops that they have something new to offer. And with companies fighting fiercely for the same market space, the mimic factor is also contributing to the huge number of new products. When one company introduces something new, you can be sure that its competitors won't be far behind with me-too products.

A Hard Road Is Now Harder

The odds of success for any new product have always been dicey. Over the years, academic and consultant studies have come up with various figures for the failure rate among new products. While estimates vary, we have yet to come across a study that didn't conclude that the *majority* of new products bomb. And we're betting that the boatloads of new products flooding the market in the past few years are making a tough situation even tougher. In Chapter 1, in fact, we'll tell you about a very interesting study done by Information Resources, Inc., a leading sales and marketing research firm, on first- and second-year new product failure rates.

Manufacturers are facing an increasingly crowded and noisy marketplace where getting new product messages heard above the competitive din is more challenging than ever before. It's an environment where the margin for error is exceedingly narrow, and the cost of making a mistake is high. It's a time when the process of planning and executing an effective new product launch has never been more difficult nor the stakes higher, for both the companies launching the new product and the people involved in the launch. After all, new products are designed to deliver revenue and profits to the bottom line, and the companies — and people — that achieve this goal are the ones that will survive and thrive.

One common response to the challenge of being heard in such an environment is to simply shout louder by spending more money on major launches. Based on the growing amount of money being shelled out for advertising each year, that may be the approach a lot of companies are adopting.

But does shouting work? We wanted to determine whether consumer products companies were reaching consumers with their launch messages, so in January 2003 we conducted the Harris Interactive®/Schneider 2002 Most Memorable New Product Launch Survey.

In this poll, we asked 4,214 adults nationwide to identify the most memorable new products of 2002. Our first question, "What were the most memorable new products of 2002?" did not include a list of new products from which to choose. Next, respondents were presented with a list of 25 products launched in 2002; the products were selected based on several factors including national distribution, uniqueness in their category, use of integrated marketing during their launch, marketing communications spending, media coverage, and product need. Aside from making the Schneider list of best products in 2002, many of the top 25 products were cited by *BusinessWeek*, *USA Today*, and *Time* in "Products of the Year" features.

The survey results were a read-it-and-weep story for marketers. Fully one-third of those polled were unable to name a single new product launched in 2002. And the news didn't get much better among the two-thirds of respondents who *could* name a new product. The highest recall figures were 7 percent for Vanilla Coke, launched in May 2002, and 5 percent for Pepsi Blue, which was introduced in July 2002. These are surprisingly unsatisfying results for two major product launches that were supported by impressive ad budgets. Vanilla Coke spent approximately 85 percent of its $24.8 million media budget beginning in May and continuing through the summer of 2002. Pepsi Blue's ad campaign, at $27.6 million, was even higher and hit during the final four months of 2002,[2] just before our survey was fielded. Prevailing wisdom holds that Pepsi Blue, at least, should still be fresh in people's minds. Once again, it seems that gaining mind share is incredibly difficult, even for America's most famous brands.

The news from our survey improved slightly when respondents were presented with a list of 25 new products and asked to pick the most memorable one. Vanilla Coke, at 19 percent, shared top honors with the MINI Cooper, which garnered 18 percent. Listerine PocketPaks came in a close third at 13 percent. But none of the remaining 22 products were mentioned by more than 7 percent of respondents. And these were products that came from brand all-stars like Campbell Soup, Heinz, Sony Ericsson, and Hanes, which spent millions to introduce their latest new product phenomena.

After reviewing the results of the study, we thought perhaps 2002 just wasn't a standout year for new product introductions. So we repeated the study in 2003 and collected 1,000 consumer responses to an on-line survey conducted by Insight Express. We increased the number of new products tested from 25 to 38 to see if including more products would improve the recall rate. This time, 50 percent of the people we polled could not name a single product that was launched in 2003. Comparing the 2002 and 2003 survey results shows that consumer recall dropped by 17 percent from one year to the next. This is not a heartwarming trend.

The news improved in 2003 when survey participants were asked which new products they recognized from a list of products launched during the year. The new $20 bill had the highest recognition factor; three out of four participants knew about it, a level that far exceeded any other new product launch of 2003.

Three other products had awareness ratings higher than 50 percent: Crest® Night Effects™ (58 percent), Claritin® OTC (54 percent), and Campbell's® Chunky M'm! M'm! Good! To Go soup (51 percent). The rest of the products ranking in the top 10 all achieved recognition ratings of over 30 percent, with four of them earning ratings of over 40 percent.

These aided-recall results made 2003 a far better year than 2002 for memorable new product launches. But the fact that 50 percent of consumers were unable to name a single new product without being prompted by a list still lingers in our minds as an unacceptable result for the billions of dollars spent on new product launches.

Create Smarter, More Powerful Launches

If your company has a new product ready to bring to market, everything we've said so far will surely produce nervous stomachs, heated discussions during launch planning sessions, and perhaps more than a few sleepless nights. Obviously, to make your consumer offering stand out in the new product stampede, you have to be more strategic than ever before.

Assuming that you've done your homework and you have a product that not only fills a market need but does it well, you still need a well-thought-out launch plan supported by perfect execution. Without such a plan and the discipline to execute it with rigor, even the best new products can die an untimely death.

So what's the secret to developing smarter, more powerful new product launches that make it through the marketing maelstrom? This was the question we attempted to answer in the Schneider/Boston University New Product Launch Report, a breakthrough study that examined how marketers launch new products and identified launch success factors.

As far as we can determine, this qualitative and quantitative study marks the first time anyone has rigorously examined how managers carry out launches in order to identify launch success factors — the strategies, tactics, and processes likely to improve the launch effort. Funded by Schneider & Associates, the project was a joint academic and research effort conducted by the Communication Research Center at Boston University in conjunction with Prescott & Associates, a strategic marketing and research firm in Pittsburgh, Pennsylvania. Susan Fournier, Ph.D., who was then associate professor of business administration/marketing at Harvard Business School, was a consultant to the study. (Fournier is currently at the Tuck School of Business at Dartmouth University.)

What You'll Learn

In this book, you'll discover the 10 key factors that separate successful launches from the also-rans, as identified in the Schneider/Boston University New Product Launch Report. You'll learn about planning, timing, team formation, leadership, budget, and strategy selection — all the things that can help boost your launch success rate. Here's what else is contained in the pages to come:

- We'll present a new model for developing launches, including our recommendation to add a seventh Launch Gate to the popular Stage-Gate® Process used by many consumer packaged goods companies. Created by Robert Cooper, Ph.D., the

Stage-Gate Process is one of the well-established roadmaps that consumer companies use for their new product development process. We'll discuss each phase of the Schneider Launch Stage-Gate model in depth so you can master this strategy for looking at launch.

- You'll discover how to ignite your launch team's creativity with a unique problem-solving process that will help you develop truly breakthrough launch ideas.
- We'll present case studies that illustrate good launch practices in action. You'll also discover how some launches have gone awry and the important lessons that these disasters offer.
- Throughout the book, we've scattered dozens of **Launch Lessons** from top marketing professionals across the country. These pithy nuggets of advice are the perfect pick-me-up when you're starting to feel your launch is stuck.
- Finally, we'll give you advice on how to avoid the trap of doing the same old thing with your launches and expecting a different result. At today's frenetic pace, no company can afford to become complacent about its launch techniques.

The Best/Worst of Times

Being part of the team that is launching a new product can be exhilarating. After all, what's more exciting than presenting your "baby" to what you hope will be a crowd of adoring customers?

But for obvious reasons, it can also be a very stressful time.

What if customers don't think your new baby is cute? (It happens! Think Edsel.) What if they think your baby costs too much? What if their lives are really hectic and they don't need another baby? What if they're so busy paying attention to all the other new babies that yours gets ignored? What if they're disappointed because your baby doesn't behave as well as you've led them to believe it will?

It's up to you to answer these questions. Our basic premise is that you've developed and correctly priced a product that fills a consumer need, that your product works properly, and has one or more new characteristics you can defend. We've written this book to help you develop and execute a launch plan that will get your new product the attention it deserves.

Now, join us in Section 1, where we define our terms and offer an in-depth look at why achieving launch success is such a struggle.

LAUNCH: AN INCREASINGLY COMPLEX CHALLENGE

Let's make sure we're all on the same page from the get-go by defining exactly what a new product launch is. We'll also discuss the myriad factors that make it essential to unveil your new consumer product with a well-planned and executed launch.

1

COMING TO TERMS WITH TERMS

A **funny thing happened** on our way to writing a book about new product launches. The more people we talked to, the more we realized that different people mean different things when they say "new product launch."

We asked people to tell us about their all-time great, innovative new product launches and what made them so successful. The next thing you know, they'd started talking about how their company came up with a new way to use an existing product and how successful that "new product" was in the marketplace. Or they'd tell us about a launch designed to reposition an existing brand or company. Others told us how they put an old product into an innovative package and then watched as sales skyrocketed, breathing new life into an icon brand. One person even talked about introducing a creative and hugely successful cause-related marketing program that garnered attention for a "suite of new products."

"Was that really a new product launch?" we'd ask.

"I think so," came the answer but sometimes in a tentative voice that made us wonder if anyone really understood just what constitutes a "new product."

The more we listened, the more we realized that the first thing we needed to do was to define what we mean by "new products." Based on our discussions with industry, agency, and media pros, we've opted for the "big tent" definition of what it means to be a new product.

When we say new product, we're talking about:

- Breakthrough technologies

- Line extensions that stretch or renew the appeal of existing products

- Brand extensions that take a franchise into a new product category

- Seasonal or holiday products that need to be relaunched each year

- The relaunch of icon products

- The relaunch of a company that is significantly shifting its focus

- The introduction of new packaging or a new feature that makes age-old products easier to use

- A new application for an existing product that will attract a totally new market segment or prompt existing customers to use the product more frequently

- Products that are new to your company but not new to the world

- An exciting cause-related program that brings new attention (and market share) to your brand

Then, when we went looking for a definition of new product launch, we were stumped. After some exhaustive research, we decided that if you want something done well, you have to do it yourself. So we did:

Launch is a powerful, multidisciplinary process that successfully propels a new product or service into the marketplace ... and sustains it over time.

Our emphasis in this book is on the "multidisciplinary" and "sustains it over time" parts of the definition. We want to pinpoint the processes that will help you craft a multipronged marketing approach, providing rapid liftoff and sales as well as long-lasting staying power.

How Did This Get So Complicated?

Defining the term "new product" was simpler in the 1950s and '60s, when life itself was simpler. Back then, there were only two kinds of new products: totally new ideas that we'd never seen before (think transistor radios, color television, hula hoops) and products that came in packages with big starbursts proclaiming "new and improved" (think detergents, cleaners, toothpaste). But now, with so many different types of products labeled "new," the lines are blurred for both consumers and marketers.

No matter what definition they use, companies today are chasing newness at warp speed. The 2004 New Product Development Survey conducted by *Stagnito's New Products Magazine* found that some small food and beverage companies (annual revenues of less than $10 million) are agile enough to go from idea to launch in as little as 22 weeks. Imagine that — someone has an idea, and five and a half months later it's being shipped out the plant door. For larger companies, product development takes longer, but even companies with revenues of $100 million to $1 billion rolled out their slowest projects in under 11 months. No wonder the number of new products is going up and up and up.[1]

This rapid pace might imply that companies have honed the new product development process to a science as they turn out an endless array of successful products. But unfortunately, that's far from true. Faster only seems to result in more new products, not better new products. In fact, according to a comprehensive study conducted in 2000 by Information Resources, Inc. (IRI), a leading sales and marketing research firm serving the consumer goods industry, manufacturers are getting it right less than 50 percent of the time.

> **"Some brands make a mistake** by bringing out something that is too much of a disparity from the norm of that brand. They think it's a good line extension, but from a consumer or trade standpoint, it doesn't make sense. When you ask them for research that outlines all the potential, those models don't exist. The mistake is extending the brand beyond the core competency. You often see this with fashion brands that have positioning in one area. Take shoes, for example. If you have a great position in comfort but not fashion, oftentimes you're better off with a new brand if you're going after the fashion market."
>
> — *Chris Donnelly, President of GeigerDonnelly Marketing LLC, Foxboro, Massachusetts*

IRI looked at 21 categories of packaged goods in which they identified 608 new products. Just over 200 of the launches were labeled "major introductions," defined as a totally new brand name or a brand extension into a new category. The remainder were classified as "minor introductions," defined as flavor or form extensions of an existing brand (but excluding new package sizes). Each of the products analyzed had been on the market long enough for IRI to gather two full years of sales data.

Fifty-two percent of the 608 new products failed to meet the study's benchmarks for success. Those benchmarks were:

- Obtaining "threshold" distribution in year one. By this measure, a product was labeled a failure if it achieved less than 50 points of distribution in its first year out of a possible 300 points (100 each for supermarket, drug, and mass merchandise outlets).

- Retaining distribution through the end of year two. By this measure, losing 30 percent or more of year-one distribution in year two put the product into the failure category.

Sales figures weren't used as benchmarks because the threshold of success for sales differs from one product category to another and from one manufacturer to another. For example, a new product with year-one sales of $10 million might be considered a success by a small manufacturer or in a small category, while those same results would be deemed a failure by a large manufacturer or in a large category.

Interestingly, IRI found no significant difference in failure rates between major and minor introductions. Fifty percent of the major introductions failed, compared with 53 percent of the minor introductions. Of the products that failed, 65 to 75 percent bit the dust in the first year. In addition, while most new products tended to see sales declines after their introductory bubble burst, successes tended to report sales increases in year two.

We also noted that success was more common among products where ad spending was higher. Seventy-five percent of the products with first-year ad spending of more than $5 million were successful. Only 32 percent of products with $1 million or less in ad support succeeded.

According to Valerie Skala, vice president of analytic product management and development at IRI, "It is likely that some of the failures were recognized by their manufacturers as having low sales potential and thus not worth significant ad support, whereas prelaunch research probably identified the successes as having large enough sales potential to merit advertising investment. In other words, the ad spending was determined by the products' predicted sales, rather than the sales being determined by the products' level of advertising support. That being said, other research does prove that a strong advertising campaign can make a significant contribution to a new product's year-one sales. IRI commonly sees advertising contributing 10 to 20 percent or more of a new product's year-one sales."

Incrementality and Sustainability

The IRI study highlights several important realities of today's new product marketplace. First, achieving incremental sales growth for a parent brand or a manufacturer is the real challenge for new product developers. Second, sustainability is a major stumbling block for many new products.

Let's discuss incrementality as IRI defines it: the percentage of a new product's sales that represents new sales for the parent brand or manufacturer as opposed to cannibalization, which is the percentage of a new product's sales that simply shifts from one item in the line to another. Retailers care about this topic: They want incremental sales because that contributes to total category growth, something they strive to obtain.

As Valerie Skala points out, achieving incremental sales growth or category growth is difficult because so many consumer product categories are highly saturated and have low growth potential. In mature markets, the danger of having your new product cannibalize the sales of existing products is great. And even if you're in a product category that hasn't reached maturity, if all you're doing is adding line extensions that don't offer consumers a new benefit, your chances of attracting incremental sales are iffy.

An ACNielsen study that evaluated the performance of 80 line extension launches found that nearly 25 percent failed to grow the total franchise. ACNielsen identified four main factors that prevent line extensions from being incremental:

- **SUBSTITUTABILITY:** The least incremental line extensions are products that consumers believe are highly substitutable for the parent brand. On the other hand, products that were more differentiated from the other products in the brand franchise provide a better opportunity for overall brand growth.

- **TRANSACTION SIZE:** Line extensions that come in smaller sizes or that generate fewer units purchased per occasion than the parent brand will not produce incremental growth.

• **BORROWED MARKETING:** ACNielsen found that the more money borrowed from the parent brand's marketing budget to support the line extension's launch, the greater likelihood that the line extension will cannibalize the parent brand.

• **STOLEN DISTRIBUTION:** The line extensions that grow the overall brand are those that gain incremental distribution. If retailers elect to replace some of the parent brand's SKUs on the shelf with the new line extension's SKUs, that is unlikely to produce incremental sales growth for the overall brand.[2]

IRI also has looked at the cannibalization trap and identified several other ways manufacturers have generated incremental sales growth:

• Creating new product categories that address an important consumer need (e.g., disposable baby bibs, men's toiletries).

• Introducing new items that are carefully designed to extend the brand's appeal to a new group of consumers, without losing sight of the brand's core equity (e.g., Gatorade reaching down to younger kids with a smaller bottle and flavors formulated to appeal to them, and Capri Sun reaching up to older kids with its Big Pouch size). Not everyone succeeds with this approach, however. Gerber's attempt to extend its baby food for adult consumption as a snack, for example, failed because they lost touch with their core equity: Gerber equals baby, and adults don't want to eat baby food. In this instance, the company

would have been better off launching an entirely new brand rather than trying to stretch what Gerber means to consumers.

• Introducing new items that deliver obviously superior performance and encourage consumers to trade up, driving increased dollar sales and profits if not unit sales (e.g., Gillette's Mach 3 and Venus razors).

As the IRI study shows, achieving sustainability for a new product is another serious challenge. According to IRI's estimates, in general, two-thirds of people who try a new product typically won't repurchase it.* Some of those one-time buyers are just variety seekers — always looking for something new, willing to try anything if the deal incentive is big enough — and they aren't prone to becoming loyal customers. Other one-time buyers will not find the new product any better than their old favorite and will revert to habit, buying what they've always bought. Psychological research has shown that adages such as "Old habits die hard" and "Habit is second nature" are true, even when it comes to something as mundane as picking a bottle of dishwashing liquid off the supermarket shelf.

In the end, you're relying on the roughly one-third of first-time buyers who make a second (repeat) purchase of your new product to keep coming back often enough to sustain a sales rate that keeps your product in its position on retail shelves. This is why many products enjoy supersonic starts — driven by the initial trial — and then crash and burn, with a dwindling "depth of repeat" (the percentage of two-time buyers who buy a third time, then the percentage of three-time buyers who buy a fourth time, and so on).

According to Valerie Skala, "There is tremendous pressure for retail shelf space, so if your product falls into the bottom third of all SKUs in terms of store sales, you're constantly in danger of losing your shelf space to another new product. And if a product doesn't remain on the shelf for at least two years, it will probably not pay back its development and launch costs, as it generally takes one to two years for a new product to reach break-even."

In evaluating a new product and whether it can achieve sustainability, Skala recommends looking at the time period consumers need to make enough purchases to become loyal users. For most products, that's three to five purchases. "Decide if you have the resources to achieve sustainability, and identify the things you can do over time to maintain interest in the product," Skala said. "This means everything from creating a marketing budget that spans two years, to introducing a steady stream of new SKUs so consumers have new reasons to repurchase the

*Keep in mind that metrics for success can vary significantly across different categories and types of products, so this statement is a broad generalization that may not apply to your category.

brand, to advertising that reminds consumers to use up the product that's sitting in their cupboard."

Figuring out how to keep a launch alive — to achieve sustainability — is a must. Throughout the book, we'll discuss numerous ways to accomplish this goal

The best way to achieve sustainability, of course, is to offer consumers an incredible new product whose brand can be built and extended over time. If a new product is poorly thought out, badly designed, or improperly priced, or it offers no real benefits over existing products, even the largest launch marketing budget won't help it survive. Consumers vote with their pocketbooks. You may get them to buy something once because the product or the launch intrigues them, but they won't buy it again unless it meets a real need. Remember all the blue food introduced in 2002? Moms bought it once based on their kids' "pester power," but the blue period ended quickly when youngsters tired of blue oatmeal, cookies, and cereal.

We can assure you this book is not a panacea for launching mediocre products, nor does it offer any miracle cures for products with no hope of achieving long-term success. While a larger budget may help propel a good product to success, even the biggest budget won't do much for an inferior product.

In the end, you'll need a first-class new product to make your launch strategy worth the cost and hard work it will take to overcome the challenges of a 21st-century launch. The next four chapters take a closer look at exactly what those challenges are.

2

LAUNCH HURDLES — THE PEOPLE FACTOR

f competing with thousands of other new products and services each year doesn't raise your blood pressure, consider the trends altering the world your new product is entering:

- Rapidly increasing diversity in the U.S. population

- Significant media proliferation

- New technologies that make it simple for viewers to ignore TV advertising

- Greater segmentation among retail channels and the resulting changes in consumer shopping habits

- Growing popularity of the Internet both for shopping and as a primary news source

- Shift of power away from manufacturers and toward retailers, particularly big box retailers

This is only a partial list of the external hurdles that stand between your new product and a successful launch. And the list changes every year, as do the tastes and preferences of consumers. Keeping abreast of these potential obstacles is an essential part of your launch planning process, so let's examine these topics and how they might impact a new product launch.

Fast-Forward Diversity and Aging

When the results of the 2000 census were released, there was such a deluge of interesting data that consumer product marketers found it difficult to decide what to focus on first. Here are some of the more thought-provoking highlights:

- The country's population diversified faster in the 1990s than in the previous decade, with minorities now accounting for one-third of the 281 million people in the United States, up from one-quarter in 1990.

- In the 1990s, the total population grew by 18 percent. That rate was seriously eclipsed by the 60 percent growth rate among Hispanics and the 48 percent growth rate among Asian Americans. The growth rate for African Americans was 16 percent.

- More than one in eight persons in the United States is now of Hispanic origin. By mid-century, one in four Americans is projected to be Hispanic.

- The racial breakdown by age suggests that racial diversification won't slow down anytime soon. Non-Hispanic whites accounted for about 69 percent of the population overall, a drop of 6.9 percent during the 1990s. In the under-18 age group, however, the percentage of non-Hispanic whites was significantly lower, at 61 percent. Among the 6.8 million who identified themselves as multiracial, 49 percent were in the under-18 age group.

- The nation's ethnic populations have more economic clout than ever before. According to the Selig Center for Economic Growth at the University of Georgia, the buying power of Hispanics will hit $1,014.2 billion by 2008 — an incredible 357 percent jump from what it was in 1990. Also by 2008, the combined buying power of African Americans, Asian Americans, and Native Americans will exceed $1.5 trillion, a 231 percent gain.[1]

- Diversity is booming among the nation's elderly population as well, with Hispanics making up the fastest-growing ethnic segment. Hispanic senior citizens are projected to increase from about 2 million in 2000 to nearly 5 million in 2020. By that year, 22 percent of those age 65 and older will belong to a racial or ethnic minority, up from 16.5 percent in 2000.

- In 2000, 35 million Americans were age 65 and older, representing 12.4 percent of the total population. This group is expected to climb to 54 million in 2020 and to more than double by 2050.

- People 85 and older make up the fastest-growing segment of the older population, and this segment is expected to grow more quickly than any other age group. In fact, this group could increase from about 4 million in 2000 to 19 million by 2050.

- The poverty rate among Americans age 65 and older was 10.2 percent in 2000. That's a considerable drop from the 35 percent poverty rate among elder Americans in 1960, when senior citizens suffered from a higher poverty rate than that of children (27 percent) or working-age people (17 percent). Today, the relative poverty rate of the older U.S. population is similar to that of working-age people and lower than that of children, 16 percent of whom live in poverty.

- In 2000, the average income among those age 65 and older was $20,851, up from $12,239 in 1974. (Figures adjusted for inflation.) A significant disparity in income exists between the genders, however. The average income for elderly men was $28,597, while for elderly women it was only $15,197. This gap should narrow, however, as working baby boomer women enter their senior years. These women will have pensions and other retirement plans that, for the most part, weren't part of the income of earlier female generations.

- The U.S. population includes an increasing number of nontraditional households, as the number of people who never marry grows, the average age at marriage climbs, and the number of single-parent households skyrockets. The percentage of unmarried females age 15 and older rose from 38 percent in 1970 to 46 percent in 2002, and the percentage of unmarried males age 15 and older grew from 32 percent to 43 percent in the same time frame. In addition, between 1970 and 2000, the number of households consisting of one person living alone increased from 17 percent to 26 percent. In short, it's not a "Leave It to Beaver" nation any more.

The Three Americas

In March 2004, award-winning Newhouse News Service reporter Jonathan Tilove pointed out in a four-part series that understanding America's demographic shifts doesn't necessarily equate to comprehending what's happening nationwide. It's critical to recognize how these changes are playing out in different parts of the country, helping to create "three Americas that look, feel and think less and less alike. It is a national metamorphosis, epic in scope, profound in its implications," wrote Tilove.[2] The three Americas that Tilove described are:

- **THE MELTING POT:** Incorporating the large urban areas where most immigrants arrive plus all of Texas, California, and New Mexico, the Melting Pot is the most multicultural place on Earth. Unprecedented waves of immigration from non-European countries have made the Melting Pot less white and more diverse at a pace without precedent. Between 1980 and 2000, the white percentage of the population in the nation's four largest Melting Pot cities — New York City; Chicago, Illinois; Los Angeles, California; and Houston, Texas — fell precipitously. Forty percent of the nation's population lives in the Melting Pot, but that pot contains 70 percent of the nation's foreign-born population.[3]

- **THE NEW SUN BELT:** Even though the fast-growing states in the Southeast and the non-California West account for only a fifth of the country's population, they are home to 79 percent of all growth in the white population. Tilove labels this America the "new suburb." He points out that in the past people moved from a city to a nearby suburb, but now "more and more people just keep going. In the 1990s, for the first decade in California's history, many more people left the state than arrived from the rest of America, which explains why the five fastest-growing states in the nation were Idaho, Utah, Colorado, Arizona and Nevada."[4]

- **THE HEARTLAND:** Made up of the Midwest minus Chicago, New England minus Boston, the Northeast minus New York City, and parts of the South that are, as Tilove puts it, "still more William Faulkner than Ted Turner,"[5] this America has been less touched by migration and immigration. In this America, at least 65 percent of the people were born in the state where they now reside; in the other two Americas, less than 65 percent of the people are native to the states in which they now live.[6]

"These migration patterns are not happening willy-nilly," demographer William Frey, of the University of Michigan and the Brookings Institution, told Tilove. "They are directed, they are persistent, and they are self-perpetuating, with each flow bringing together more people with similar backgrounds and interest and common goals. They will indelibly shape the future of our politics, our relations between the races and generations and, in the end, our sense of nationhood. People in each of these Americas will have a different idea of what America is."[7]

Understanding the distinctions among these three very different Americas is vital to small and regional companies that may be operating wholly within one region, as well as to large companies conducting nationwide launches. As these immigration and migration trends proceed apace, it will be more difficult — and more critical — than ever before to develop launch plans and messages that truly speak to specific markets. Launch campaigns will have to become more targeted and more multilayered (i.e., with launch segments that appeal to all three Americas) to speak to these increasingly distinct consumer populations.

Implications for New Product Launches

There's certainly no lack of changes to assimilate into your future launch planning. How do you translate these interesting factoids into meaningful guidance for your next product launch? We believe the most compelling take-away lesson is that the American market is undergoing a dramatic demographic morphing.

The increase in population diversity means a one-size-fits-all launch strategy will no longer work for new consumer products that need to reach a wide range of the population to succeed. Perhaps 20 years ago you could get away with developing one launch message for your mainly white, young, or working-age target audience, but today you need to take a segmented approach that enables you to reach diverse audiences. And this multiple-messages-for-multiple-audiences methodology will become more crucial with each passing year.

On the other hand, if you have a new product meant for a specific ethnic population, the growth of America's major ethnic groups, along with their mushrooming buying power, means you have more potential customers than ever before. Thanks to the proliferation of ethnic media, which we'll talk about shortly, you can develop a highly focused effort that reaches your target audience in ways never before possible. At the same time, you should consider whether other ethnic populations might also be ripe for your new product, and design launch efforts specifically for them.

With growing numbers of people in each ethnic group, the potential payoff for investing in a customer base within every community expands substantially. And because ethnic groups tend to be very brand loyal, inviting them into your family of brands often means they become customers for life. African Americans, for example, are four times more brand loyal than the general market, and Hispanics are two times more brand loyal, according to Robert McNeil, Jr., chief executive officer and founder of IMAGES USA, a multicultural marketing communications firm in Atlanta, Georgia.

Finally, the relative affluence of the rapidly growing elderly population opens up new opportunities for companies to consider targeting their products to this age group. Perhaps it's time to shed the outdated practice of spending 95 percent of marketing and advertising budgets on those under age 50.[8] Today's senior citizens — and the 76 million baby boomers that will enter the senior citizen category starting in 2011 — are healthier, wealthier, better educated, and more active than previous generations of seniors. Finding a way to make your new product attractive to this group will significantly boost your chances of success. And because both of these groups are expected to live longer than previous generations did, captivating these consumers means higher product sales for decades to come.

3

LAUNCH HURDLES —
BEHAVIORAL TRANSFORMATIONS

If **adapting a launch campaign** to shifting U.S. demographics isn't nerve-wracking enough, marketers also have to stay on top of significant changes in consumer behaviors and attitudes in the post-millennium, post-9/11 world. According to J. Walker Smith, president of Yankelovich Partners, a branding and marketing consultancy specializing in lifestyle trends and customer targeting solutions, "Marketers are facing a period of transition in which more change in consumer values [is taking place] than at any point since the early 1970s; huge value changes are occurring."[1] In a December 2003 article on the addition of trend-tracking specialists at several of the leading U.S. ad firms, *The New York Times* noted, "As changes in demographics and

> "It's amazing how clients** hold back on doing qualitative research that would help us [the advertising agency] get in the mind of consumers and learn about their priorities and their views of the product benefits, to help us fine-tune our launch messages. Clients are reticent to spend that money because they think they know the customer. They overlook this small investment in account planning that could yield valuable results."
>
> — *Scott Russell, Chief Marketing Officer of MRA Group, Syracuse, New York, and Philadelphia, Pennsylvania*

lifestyles accelerate, consumer behavior is becoming increasingly difficult to predict."[2]

Forecasting how consumers will react to your new product and its launch campaign is exactly what you want to do, so news of major shifts in consumer values and less predictable consumer behavior is troubling information. Ignoring changes in consumer thinking and lifestyles is perilous if not downright foolhardy. Let's take a look at some thought-provoking trends in the consumer behavior and attitude arena:

- In their book *Trading Up,* authors Michael Silverstein, senior vice president of the Boston Consulting Group, and Neil Fiske, chief executive officer of Bath & Body Works, say American consumers in the middle market (i.e., the 48 million households with incomes of $50,000-plus) are choosing to buy what they have labeled the "New Luxury" products and services.

There's a duality to this trend that's important to understand: At the same time consumers are trading up to products that deliver higher levels of quality, taste, and aspiration, they are also trading down on commodity items. As Silverstein and Fiske note, the same woman who willingly plunks down a hefty $28 for a Victoria's Secret bra will hit the local Costco or Sam's Club for commodity goods.

- The VIP culture, in which consumers crave a sense of exclusivity, is another trend worth watching. Credit card companies have long tapped into this consumer desire with gold and platinum-level cards; now other marketers are catching up. "It's about having a backstage pass, separating yourself from everyone else," said Zoe Lazarus, managing director of Ogilvy & Mather Worldwide's new trend-watching division. "The more everything becomes accessible, the more some people want to be separate, desire status and prestige."[3] As examples of marketer responses to the VIP culture trend, Lazarus cites limited edition merchandise from clothing manufacturers, V.V.I.P. rooms at clubs that are even more exclusive than V.I.P. sections, and frequent flyer programs that enable travelers to check in from their home computers and then fast track past the waiting throngs at the airport.

• Yankelovich's Smith believes we've entered the "post accumulation marketplace," in which intangibles, quality, and time have overtaken tangibles, quantity, and money as consumers' priorities. "Few marketers understand or appreciate that their rules-of-thumb about consumers are rapidly being made obsolete," Smith said. "Even the basic presumption that people shop to accumulate things is quickly becoming outdated. Indeed, people don't want to accumulate things anymore — they want intangibles, experiences and service, but no 'stuff' left over."[4]

• Less earthshaking than Smith's notion of consumers who don't want to consume are shopping behavior shifts brought on by a 24/7 world. The folks working in businesses that have to be open around the clock are so busy working that they don't have time to shop. As reported in *Facts, Figures, & the Future*, this extended workweek has led to a shift in shopping behavior. In 2003, for example, for the third year in a row Sunday was the most important shopping day in the grocery channel.[5]

• Futurist Faith Popcorn points out in a trend she labels "Mystic Messages" that religious fundamentalism is booming. With 49 percent of Americans saying they are "born again," Popcorn predicts that major marketers will finally recognize this trend and develop products and services targeting this market.

• "Burst of Energy" is what trend analyst Ellen Ratchye-Foster, founder of Burning Glass Consulting, calls people's desire to escape from everyday pressures with a jolt of pure adrenaline. Ratchye-Foster, who provides insights for Fallon Worldwide and other clients, says people are even looking for the emotional relief provided by a quick temper tantrum, which may explain the appeal of "bad boy" actors like Colin Farrell. "For brands, this phenomenon creates some risks since volatility is the antithesis of good branding," she says. "But this is a good time to not take oneself too seriously; it's a good time to have a sense of humor about who you are and what you do and who you aren't and what you don't do."

• Another trend that Ratchye-Foster sees is hope. "Despite the stresses and strains of the last few years including personal, political, and global, almost every polling question posed to consumers results in a positive view," she notes. "This should cause marketers to think about how to offer hope to customers and how to demonstrate hope and faith in a brand and in a company."

• Neighborhood pride is making a big comeback, with renewed interest in local identities right down to individual city districts and suburbs, according to Ogilvy & Mather's Lazarus. "This is interesting for brands that have placed so much emphasis on global strategies, but now need to recognize there's also local pride,"[6] she said.

• Perhaps tying in with neighborhood pride is "hiving," the name the Yankelovich team has given to a trend that represents engagement, interaction, and connection with the outside environment from the home environment or "hive." Instead of cocooning as people did in the 1980s and 1990s, when they went home and shut the door on the outside world, consumers now are seeking connection with others in the home environment. "The return to home today is about reaching out to others," said Yankelovich's Smith. "Across all generations, family is more important than ever. People see more value in community. Through hiving, home is the best place to reestablish relationships and connect with others. Home is command central for this new lifestyle."[7]

Implications for New Product Launches

Understanding the implications of these trends and the numerous other changes that futurists predict is an important element of launch planning. Such consumer trends impact everything from product positioning to distribution channels, from media strategy to the type of launch support events you choose.

Knowing that people are taking more pride in their individual neighborhoods, for example, might spur you to take a much more grassroots approach to your launch. And being aware of the hiving trend could inspire a strategy that focuses on providing the influentials in your market with what they need to create in-home events featuring your new product (á la Pampered Chef, Mary Kay, Tastefully Simple, or Tupperware parties) as opposed to a strategy focused on launch events at public places.

Unlike the demographic trends described in Chapter 2, which are guaranteed to occur, consumer behavioral trends are completely unpredictable. Indeed, the trends described earlier may have mutated into something new and different by the time you launch your next product. Or, major new global or national events may have pushed aside these trends and created totally new ones. Constant research is essential for keeping track of what's happening now that might impact your launch.

Contemplating these consumer behavioral changes should spark out-of-the-box thinking among launch team members. In fact, what these trends show is that the box itself (i.e., consumer behavior and attitudes) is changing. The savvy launch team will interact with their target consumers where they live, work, and play so that it's clear which trends are impacting their markets. By understanding which launch strategies will be in sync with consumer lifestyles and attitudes — today and tomorrow — the team will be able to craft a launch campaign that resonates with their target audiences.

4

LAUNCH HURDLES —
MEDIA FOR EVERYONE

For companies with new products to launch, developments in the media world offer both good news and bad news. Let's take a look at key media industry trends that will bear watching as you plan your launch:

• The average American household can receive roughly 180 television channels. As *Plunkett's Entertainment & Media Industry Almanac* points out, "This trend puts advertisers, rather than media companies, in the driver's seat with regard to advertising rates and purchasing trends. If one media outlet's rates are excessive, then there are a growing number of alternatives for advertisers to turn to."[1]

• While far more TV channels are available today, the key audience for new product launches watches less television than the general population. The 21 million so-called "influentials" that Roper ASW, a marketing research and consulting firm, says shape national opinions and trends, are far less likely than the norm to watch TV. Only 35 percent of this group reports watching TV "often," 14 percent lower than the total public. Seventy-seven percent of influentials say they watch TV "occasionally," 11 percent lower than the total public.[2]

• Digital video recorders (DVRs) such as TiVo and Replay are making it possible for people to decide when they want to watch their favorite TV shows and, of great significance to advertisers, enabling them to skip commercials. In fact, the technology has proven so attractive that cable companies are rapidly adapting it with DVR-ready set-top boxes that are simple and cheaper to use than standalone products. The Yankee Group, a technology forecasting company, estimates that in four years, almost 25 million homes will have DVR capability.[3]

> **"Using advertising too soon is** one of the big mistakes people make with launches. A good example is XM Satellite Radio. They spent $100 million on advertising in its first year and $70 million in its second year. Now the product is trying to take off, and they have no money left for advertising. They spent all their advertising money upfront, when it didn't do any good because the product didn't have credibility yet. Once you've achieved credibility, then you need to do advertising to get people to sign up, but in this case, they've spent their advertising dollars already."
>
> — Al Ries, Chairman of Ries & Ries, Atlanta, Georgia, and author of The Fall of Advertising & the Rise of PR

• Forty-seven percent of the 45.1 million adults who have both a TV and a computer in the same room reported that they frequently use the Internet while watching television. Another 29 percent said they multitasked in this fashion occasionally.[4]

• Also on the TV front, *The New York Times* in 2003 reported on an Initiative Media study that showed the viewing habits of black and white households have become more similar over the past decade. "Of the 20 prime-time series watched most by blacks in the fourth quarter (of 2002), the survey reported, nine were also among the 20 most watched by whites," according to *The New York Times*.[5]

• The number of consumer magazines has tripled in the past 20 years and now stands at about 5,500.[6] From *All About Beer* to *Herb Companion*, from *Wyoming Homes and Living Magazine* to *Crafty Kids*, there is a publication to reach literally anyone anywhere. The same holds true for cable channels, where ever-narrower audience segments are being pursued.

• Spanish-language media are expanding at a rapid pace that matches the growth of the Hispanic population. Spanish-language

TV stations are top rated in some major cities, and in 2003, Spanish-language newspapers debuted or expanded in Dallas, Texas; Orlando, Florida; and Chicago, Illinois.[7] Despite this growing media availability, less than 1 percent of the hundreds of billions of dollars spent on U.S. advertising is devoted to Spanish-language media.[8] But marketers are beginning to wake up to this audience, as evidenced by the 23.7 percent growth in ad dollars devoted to Hispanic magazines in 2003.[9]

• The nation has 50 percent more radio stations than it did 30 years ago, with 10,500 stations now vying for listener attention.[10] Equally important, with the availability of Internet radio, local stations aren't just competing with local stations anymore; they're competing with stations nationwide.

• According to Nielsen//NetRatings, an Internet research firm, by the first quarter of 2004 nearly 75 percent of Americans, or 204.3 million people, had access to the Internet from home — up 9 percent from just a year ago.[11] Across all media, the Internet now ranks number three in terms of usage, according to Knowledge Networks/SRI; with a 13 percent share, the Internet lags well behind television (48 percent) and radio (31 percent), but its share jumped by 23 percent between 2002 and 2003.[12] If that trend continues, the Internet could easily leap into second place within just a few years.

• Among Internet users, 79 percent say they expect a business to have a Web site with information on products they are considering buying.[13]

• Women have now surpassed men when it comes to home Internet access. Eighty-two percent of women ages 35 to 54 access the Internet at home, compared with 80 percent of men in that age group. Among females ages 25 to 34, 76 percent surf the Web from home, while 75.6 percent of men in that age bracket have home Internet access.[14]

• Broadband Internet access in homes is growing by leaps and bounds. The number of broadband connections grew by 27 percent during the six-month period from May to November 2003, Nielsen//NetRatings reported in early 2004. This means 49.5 million people, or 38 percent of all home Internet users, now have high-speed access to the Web.

• Despite the millions of Internet sites, the actual number of news outlets that consumers are accessing is surprisingly low. Researchers at the National Center for Digital Government at Harvard University found that among the 20 most popular news sites, the top five get more traffic than the remaining 15 sites combined.[15]

• A powerful new media force is emerging on-line. Dubbed "Consumer Generated Media" by Intelliseek, a technology firm that uses the unstructured information available on the Internet to provide insights for marketers, this new media force includes discussion groups, chat rooms, and blogs. These are all places where consumers spread the word about what they like — and dislike — about products, generating the all-powerful word-of-mouth recommendations that can make or break any new product.

• Last but certainly not least, there's the issue of advertising credibility. An on-line survey conducted by Forrester Research and Intelliseek in late 2003 found that while one-third of the 470 respondents said ads influenced their purchases, a whopping 76 percent disagreed with the statement, "Companies tell the truth in ads."

Implications for New Product Launches

Clearly, the proliferation of media over the past 30 years — and especially in the past decade — shows no signs of abating. On one hand, this is positive news because it means you have greater ability than ever before to carefully target advertising and publicity to your "dream" consumer.

Yet media proliferation also presents a challenge. Long gone are the halcyon days of the 1970s, when the 90 percent share of the viewing audience that NBC, CBS, and ABC captured meant you could reach nearly every home in America just by advertising on the networks' evening news or on the most popular entertainment programs. In fact, the networks' audience share is now down to 40 percent.

Finding just the right newspapers, magazines, radio stations, cable networks, and Internet sites to target with ads and publicity is a much bigger and more critical task today. When you have to segment your TV buy, for example, you don't have the clout to arrange "special deals" with stations, thus decreasing the added value of your buy. Marketers now have to take a single budget and make it work over multiple channels, diluting the power that ad frequency provides to drive sales.

People are getting their news and information from a broad range of sources, so any launch plan that fails to take a multimedia approach risks falling flat on its face. Avoiding Spanish-language media, for example, is no longer wise. Similarly, ignoring the Internet is simply not possible, especially when ever-growing numbers of women are surfing the Web; with this population's control over household spending, finding ways to reach out to them via the Internet is becoming essential to new product success.

The good news here is that with more home users having access to broadband, marketers can use more rich media-based presentations, such as on-demand video and flash-based content, making their Internet offerings more dynamic. But along with widespread and faster access to the Internet comes the growing necessity of monitoring consumer-generated media on-line. Tracking Internet buzz, and even knowing how to influence it, is already important for new product launches. It's bound to become even more so with each passing year.

The proliferation of technology that allows consumers to completely ignore TV advertising is clearly a huge challenge to product launches. The problem stems from passive avoidance of commercials, which is what's happening with many of those people who are surfing the Internet while they watch TV. Which direction are heads turning during commercials — toward the TV set or toward the computer screen?

But the bigger threat comes as more affordable and easier-to-use forms of digital video recorders become readily available from cable and satellite companies. This technology is rapidly moving beyond the early adapter population, and growing numbers of consumers will have the ability to just say "no" to commercials, virtually eliminating a much-relied-on launch tool. Greater ingenuity will be required to come up with launch plans that reach consumers in new, more effective ways.

As Al Ries and Laura Ries point out in their bestseller, *The Fall of Advertising & the Rise of PR*, public relations is more effective than advertising for brand building and product launches. So perhaps being forced to think outside the box that sits in the living room is what's necessary now that the box isn't as cost effective.

Finally, it's impossible to ignore data showing that 995 out of the 1,000 ads a consumer sees each day are forgotten and that the vast majority of people believe companies lie in their ads. Building a launch campaign that is both credible and memorable is clearly a huge challenge for today's marketers.

5

LAUNCH HURDLES —
THE CHANNELS MAZE

Getting a new product to market isn't what it used to be, for the simple reason that the retail landscape has morphed dramatically in just the past decade alone. Rampant retail consolidation, the ever-increasing popularity of store brands, the fragmentation of channels, the advent of e-tailers — it all makes the task of setting up distribution for your new product increasingly complex. And if you're a new manufacturer or a small to mid-size company, the challenge is especially daunting.

Let's look at some of the major developments that are making it hard to navigate through the channel maze:

• Major consolidation within the retail industry, along with Wal-Mart's emergence as a behemoth

> **"Packaging is the absolute** most critical feature to trial today. The average consumer spends less than 2.9 seconds to eyeball a package, a minuscule amount of time. If the package doesn't grab and catch them, that is your first hurdle. Put together a package that screams different, unique, and fresh. The beauty shot has to jump out and say, 'I am good!'"
>
> *— Jon Rocke, President of RMH Foods, Morton, Illinois*

that controls 10 percent of total U.S. household spending[1], exemplify the serious tilt in the balance of power between manufacturers and retailers. Today, a manufacturer seeking national distribution for a new product has a limited number of retailers to whom he can pitch a product.

• Retail channels are fragmented as never before, taking channel management to a whole new level. When you're launching a new product nowadays, you have to consider whether it has a chance in mass retailers, super grocery stores, regular grocery stores, warehouse club stores, convenience stores, dollar stores, and drugstores. The growth of alternative channels is taking a toll on some of the more traditional channels too. For instance, the number of shopping trips to neighborhood grocery stores per week is falling.[2]

• Different channels attract different shoppers. While the woman of the household, the traditional shopper for consumer packaged goods, is still going to the grocery store, dads and teenagers prefer convenience stores. And while big box formats are still on the rise, small-box retailers that offer hurried shoppers convenience with quick and easy access are opening stores at a rapid pace.[3]

• Channel blurring is everywhere. A consumer with a craving for chocolate, for example, can now satisfy his or her sweet tooth at a wide variety of stores. Even home goods retailer Bed Bath & Beyond routinely stocks sweet treats near its checkout counters to encourage impulse purchases.

• Retailers increasingly are asking manufacturers to send them new products on an exclusive basis for lengthy introductory periods. For instance, when Jim Keyes took over as chief executive officer of 7-Eleven Inc., his strategy for bringing new life to the 21,000-store chain was to feature innovative products on the shelves. As *Brandweek* reported, Keyes "demanded his managers push suppliers for exclusive products, resulting in hits such as the zero-calorie Diet Pepsi Slurpee, Island Way Sorbet, gum from beverage maker SoBe, and the Slurpee Candy Straw developed in conjunction with Foreign Candy."[4]

• Retailers want to be brands unto themselves. John Parham, division president of media brands for Parham Santana, a New

York brand strategy and design firm, points out that this has vast implications for the types of packaging and point-of-sale materials that are acceptable to individual retailers. "You might think you're the brand," Parham said, "but in their minds, they (the retailers) are the brand."

• On-line retail sales are moving steadily higher. *The New York Times* reported that Internet sales, excluding travel and auctions, topped $50 billion in 2003, up about 22 percent from the previous year.[5]

• Private label sales are growing much faster than those of branded products. According to ACNielsen, between 1997 and 2002, private label product sales volume jumped 38 percent, double the 19 percent sales rise for branded goods.[6] Private labels are moving into more categories as well, and supermarket chains have taken them to a whole new level in terms of attractive packaging, product quality, and advertising and promotional support.

> **"Retailers are looking to be** brands unto themselves, so you have to know what the retailer will accept and what has worked in their store before. Come to them with a program that stirs things up but also takes the path of least resistance. Very seldom are you going to find success if you walk in and say, 'We expect you to redo your shelves.' You have to work backwards and know that your product will fit on the shelf. Go to the store and take photos and then say to the retailer, 'Here's a successful end cap display that is in your store right now, and we'd like to take that same configuration and overlay it with our message.' The stores want to do things the way they want to do it, and they're so powerful that you have to go with that."
>
> *— John Parham, Division President of Parham Santana, New York, New York*

• Promotional clutter in stores seems to be expanding, although some retailers have launched "clean store" policies to help contain it. Mosaic InfoForce, a leading provider of in-store data collection and retail merchandising services, found a 35 percent increase in the number of products on display in the average grocery store between 2002 and 2003 — equal to an increase of 20 displays per store. While this means more room to highlight new products, the increased clutter makes each display less effective.

Slotting Fees: The 800-Pound Gorilla

Here's something else we can blame on those dastardly cigarette companies. In 1970, cigarette manufacturers started a bidding war in which they offered to pay supermarkets a fee to place branded point-of-sale merchandisers in prime end-of-aisle locations.[7] As grocers realized that manufacturers would actually pay for shelf space, they developed so-called slotting fees. Also called slotting allowances, they're payments from manufacturers to retailers for placing new products on store shelves or in a retailer's warehouse.

Beginning in the late '70s, the concept spread rapidly to all sectors of the grocery store. Other innovative fees followed, such as failure fees, which retailers charge to remove new products from the shelves when they don't meet volume targets during their first six months. The reverse, pay-to-stay fees, keep existing products on the shelves. For retailers, these fees have become a way to combat the costs and the inherent risks of putting a new product on the shelf.

By the 1990s, the practice of charging slotting fees had become so ingrained that a U.S. Senate investigation estimated grocers were taking in $9 billion each year from such charges.[8] At some point, the practice also spread to the drugstore industry.

From the retailers' point of view, the fees make complete sense. The average supermarket today has 35,000 items.[9] Some are perennial good performers that are definitely going to retain their shelf space. That means the amount of space open for the thousands of new products being introduced each year is limited — and therefore extremely valuable to retailers and manufacturers alike. Given their small profit margin of only one penny per dollar of sales[10], retailers need to be sure they devote this limited space to products that are going to be winners. Slotting fees are one way to ensure success, because many retailers think a manufacturer's willingness to pay a slotting fee signals its belief in a new product and its commitment to helping the product succeed. In effect, the fees are a put-your-money-where-your-mouth-is message from retailers to manufacturers.

The Food Marketing Institute, a trade group for grocers and wholesalers, points out that while the use of slotting fees appears to be increasing, some of the nation's largest and fastest-growing supermarket chains, along with some regional food retailers and alternative-format retailers, do not charge slotting fees.[11] And given grocers' ever-so-slim profit margin, it's hard to make the argument that retailers are getting rich from slotting fees.

From the manufacturers' point of view, however, slotting fees have become the 800-pound gorilla of the new product launch process. The financial burden on startup or small manufacturers can be particularly onerous, although some retailers say they make allowances for small or local companies and don't charge them slotting fees. And of course, there are the consumer packaged goods giants of the industry who simply refuse to pay slotting fees on the grounds that their ad budgets, branding expertise, strong product development, and testing processes provide retailers with enough assurance that their new products will be successful.

As slotting fees have become the norm rather than the exception, they have also become controversial — so much so, in fact, that congressional committees have conducted hearings on the practice and the Federal Trade Commission has held several rounds of investigations, in 1995 and 2001. Plenty of economists and industry experts argue strongly in support of slotting fees as a legitimate mechanism to help retailers decide what to put on their limited shelf space. Others, however, contend that these fees stifle competition, raise consumer prices, and push out small manufacturers.

Since the subject of slotting fees is so controversial and the relationships between retailers and manufacturers are so veiled in secrecy, government investigators have not been able to gather enough quality data to enable either Congress or the FTC to reach any firm conclusions on slotting fees. As one indication of how hard it is to bring the needed data to light, two witnesses who appeared before a Senate panel in 1999 wore hoods to hide their identities because they feared reprisals from retailers and manufacturers.[12]

A $900,000 FTC study released in the fall of 2003 provided some interesting data, but drew no conclusions about the actual economic impact of slotting fees. The study looked at five product categories and collected information from seven national retailers, six manufacturers, and two food brokers representing manufacturers of products in the study's categories. The manufacturers who participated in the study reported that they paid slotting allowances for 80 to 90 percent of their new product introductions, at least for products that were delivered to retailers' warehouses and not directly to stores. (The report noted that fees were less likely to be charged if products were delivered directly to stores instead of to warehouses.) The manufacturers also estimated that a national rollout for a new product to be placed in 80 to 90 percent of U.S. retail grocery outlets would require $1.5 million to $2 million in slotting allowance payments.[13]

Small manufacturers and distributors that are trying to launch new products into supermarkets and drugstores tell us slotting fees are a huge hurdle. But it's not just the little guys who are impacted: A small division of one of the country's best-known consumer products companies told us they have shelved a number of innovative ideas for new products. The problem? They realized they couldn't make money after slotting fees were added in to the potential products' financial projections.

If you're a small manufacturer with limited financial resources, you're going to have to really do your homework before approaching a retailer; the impression you must create from the get-go is professionalism and confidence in the prognosis for your product. You have to present a persuasive explanation of why your product is going to succeed in its target market and a well-thought-out marketing plan that shows how you are wisely allocating your limited resources to support the product's launch. We'll talk more about overcoming the challenge of slotting fees in Chapter 21.

Implications for New Product Launches

The fragmentation in retail channels means you need a clear picture of who shops where. Each channel has a specific demographic pattern, according to research done by the Food Marketing Institute, ACNielsen, and The Lempert Report. For instance, big box retailers draw a disproportionate percentage of their heavy shopper dollar sales from large households, while convenience stores, drugstores, and club stores draw a disproportionate amount of their heavy shopper sales from smaller households.[14]

The savvy manufacturer can translate such knowledge into an opportunity to offer large-sized packages to mass retailers and grocery stores while providing smaller packages to convenience stores and drugstores.

According to Kim Feil, chief executive officer of Mosaic InfoForce, the fragmentation of retail channels is a mixed bag for manufacturers. "Each channel has its own rules and guidelines, and each retailer within that channel has its own rules and guidelines," she said. "You have to make sure you understand this matrix before you try to get in the door. For example, the dollar stores are looking for large quantities at low prices; their mantra is that low prices are critical to their metrics. If your package or price isn't the right size, you won't get distribution with them. So some manufacturers are creating smaller packages to slide in under the $1 price point. It's the classic product, price, and promotion mix. These factors might change dramatically as you move from one channel to another."

On the good news side, Feil said regional companies that don't stand a chance with Wal-Mart or Target might find success with a regional chain that big manufacturers have overlooked.

"An extremely effective new product launch strategy might be to select a few retailers who will sell your new product very effectively. Later, when you roll out in a larger market, you won't be as vulnerable as if you tried to enter all markets simultaneously," Feil said. "This flies in the face of conventional wisdom, which says to get as much distribution as fast as you can. But picking four or five channels, and giving them exclusivity in their channel or their package size, might put you ahead of the game." Of course, Feil pointed out, this strategy can backfire if other stores are angry that you haven't offered your product to them, but if consumer demand is high, even the cranky retailers will have to accept your product.

The blurring of retail channels, where items that used to be found

---

"The doors are open at most leading retailers if you can justify your visit. Most people underestimate what has to be done today to engage the distributing and retailing community for launching a product that is a commercial success. You need to talk intelligently about your business and be clear about what consumers want and need. What is the product's reason for being? What packaging will be required to make sure this product wins on the shelf? What is the promotional strategy that will enthuse consumers and engage their imaginations? You have to answer these questions for retailers."

— *Eric Baty, Chief Operating Officer of Café Bom Dia, Miami, Florida* only in one type of store are now available in other retail formats, means manufacturers may be lucky enough to find outlets beyond their traditional channels for launching new products. Learning the needs of a new retail segment adds to the complexity of a launch, but this channel blurring may help make up for the consolidation narrowing your traditional channels.

The fact that stores are seeking to be brands unto themselves also provides an opportunity to gain shelf space by offering exclusives on new products, either a total exclusive, a channel exclusive, or a more limited exclusive based on package size or some other variable.

Finally, the increase in store aisle clutter from promotional displays makes it tougher to get your marketing message about your new product across at the retail level, where the vast majority of purchasing decisions are made. As never before, the packaging on your new product has to be just right and your message has to stand out and be crystal clear.

The main lesson from all of the retail-level changes is that your distribution strategy for launching your new product needs to be more creative than ever before. In addition, distribution planning (and implementation) needs to start during your new product development process. The world is simply too complex to let this important aspect of launching your product wait until the last minute.

6

Uncovering Launch Success Factors

Now that you've looked at the many factors that make it tougher and tougher to successfully launch new products, how can you shift the odds in your favor? Finding the answer to this critical question requires understanding the launch process inside and out, which is what drove us to commission the Schneider/Boston University New Product Launch Report. In the next section, we'll start sharing what we learned in this first-ever comprehensive look at how companies conduct new product launches. But first, let's take a closer look at the study's two phases.

In the first phase, which involved qualitative research, we interviewed 10 carefully chosen launch experts from companies such as BRITA Products Co. (a subsidiary of The Clorox Co.), Royal Appliance Mfg. Co., and Unilever. The products launched by these executives each received more than two new product awards from prestigious organizations or publications. Our goal in talking with the experts in this qualitative phase was to understand the activities that made up the launch process, the tools applied, and the conventional or unconventional wisdom that guided launch activities. We analyzed the transcribed interview data, identified salient issues, developed preliminary hypotheses from these themes, and integrated the findings as inputs to the next phase of the study — the comprehensive quantitative survey.

In phase two, we surveyed consumer product executives at enterprises with annual revenues ranging from $10 million to $10 billion; the average annual revenue figure was $2.6 billion. Ninety-one executives completed our extensive and highly structured survey with responses that we found to be open, honest, thorough, and insightful.

The Survey Sample

You're probably wondering exactly what kinds of companies we surveyed. The sample of organizations in the quantitative part of the study represented a broad array of consumer product companies from industries heavily engaged in new product activities. On average, one-fifth of their organizational revenues over the past year were generated from new products. The food and beverage industry was most widely represented, with 61 percent of the total sample. Next came sporting goods with 16 percent, and apparel and shoes with 13 percent.

The study sample was largely composed of senior-level executives: Fifty-one percent held chief executive officer, senior vice president, or marketing vice president positions. Twenty-five percent were marketing directors, and 24 percent were marketing, brand, or product managers. The typical participant had managed new products for eight years and had been personally responsible for introducing an average of seven new products and 11 line extensions from planning through market launch.

To scrutinize the new product development/launch process, we asked study participants for detailed information about their most recent new product introductions. This yielded cases studies for a wide variety of product categories, including ready-to-eat breakfast cereal, refrigerated apple juice, athletic footwear, bicycles, shampoo, and wrinkle-free men's pants.

The new product cases were segmented into two groups based on in-market performance — highly successful and less successful launches. We derived the segmentation from a self-reported measure of market performance. Respondents were asked to evaluate the success of their most recent new product introduction on a 10-point scale, with 10 "an overwhelming success" and 1 "a dismal failure." Just over half (58 percent) of the executives rated their new products as being a top-three box success (i.e., a rating of 8, 9, or 10). Based on the total distribution of cases along this 10-point scale, these introductions were put into the "highly successful" category. Those with a rating of 7 or lower, representing 42 percent of the product cases, were defined as "less successful."

Using this segmentation helped us identify key drivers that led to effective new product introductions. In addition, the segmentation approach was validated by several other performance measures. For example, the two groups differed significantly in terms of performance relative to goal, a standard used to judge many product introductions. Close to three-quarters (71 percent) of the products that had been defined as highly successful outperformed the goals set for their introductions, compared with just 6 percent of the less successful products. In contrast, two-thirds (67 percent) of the managers of less successful products reported their products had performed below goals.

While complaints are often heard around corporate water coolers about the difficulty of meeting goals, 72 percent of the executives surveyed said the goals set for their particular new product introduction were realistic. Marketers with less successful products were significantly more likely to believe their goals were set too high (39 percent versus 12 percent of those with highly successful products). We found both these statistics interesting from a sociological point of view, since those who succeeded said the benchmarks were fair and those who didn't succeed were crying the blues — typical responses from winners and losers.

Now, let's start looking at the findings of our research study, including the 10 launch strategies that can help guide your new product to success.

TIMING AND PLANNING
FACTORS

Some of the most important launch success factors uncovered in the Schneider/Boston University New Product Launch Report relate to timing and planning. In this section, we'll share the four critical lessons we learned about timing and planning, including the concept of treating launch as a separate, distinct phase of the new product development process.

7

Is Timing Everything?

Think for a minute about how your company treats new product launches. Have you defined a separate, distinct launch phase within the new product development process? Have you specifically identified when planning should start for this launch phase? How about when launch activities should end?

If your answer to all three questions is "Yes," then our response is, "Congratulations! You have already taken major steps toward assuring that your new product launch will succeed!"

Sad to say, we learned during the Schneider/Boston University launch study that if you can answer "yes" to these questions, you're in the minority. Only 44 percent of the executives in the study reported that their organizations map out a distinct product launch phase. In contrast, 56 percent considered launch to be merely the culmination of the product development process.

This result immediately raised red flags for us. We worried that if companies don't think of launch as a separate phase, odds are they aren't giving it the amount of time and attention it deserves. At these companies, launch may be in danger of becoming an afterthought, with planning activities starting too late to produce the forecasted results.

In fact, our suspicions were confirmed as we delved deeper into our research. First, we found that highly successful products were slightly more likely to have been introduced by organizations that viewed launch as a separate phase. Among the highly successful launches included in the study, 51 percent came from companies that viewed launch as separate and distinct.

But it was among the less successful products in the study that this factor really stood out. Of the executives who labeled their new products as "less successful," only 32 percent said their organizations viewed launch as a separate phase. This means 68 percent of the companies that were disappointed with the success of their new products had failed to adopt the launch-is-its-own-phase methodology.

Launch Strategy #1:
Treat Launch As a Separate Phase

Our results indicate that if you don't already give launch its due by treating it as a separate phase, it's time to change your thinking. Doing so forces you to consider critical questions and to seize control of important timing factors, such as when planning for launch should begin and when it should end. The more deliberate you are in scheduling and handling launch, the better your results are bound to be.

Where Does Launch Fit?

Now, if launch should be a separate, distinct phase of the new product development process, the question is where to place it within the entire spectrum. To get a better handle on this, we asked our study respondents a series of questions related to the new product development process as a whole.

For these companies, that process generally begins three or more years before shipment and often continues until the two to three months leading up to launch. We identified four subprocesses in the new product development cycle:

1. INITIAL CONCEPT GENERATION — This subprocess usually begins at least one or two years prior to shipment.

2. FINAL PRODUCT DEVELOPMENT — Usually completed

two or three months prior to shipment, this subprocess is generally concurrent with the timing of a final go/no-go decision on the product.

3. CONCEPT AND PRODUCT TESTING — This can start within one or two years after initiation of the product development phase and may last almost up to shipment. This subprocess generally runs hand in hand with the development of a prototype and a final product.

4. LAUNCH — This subprocess generally starts one or two years prior to shipment of the final product.

One unexpected finding from our questions in this area was that concept development began far earlier for the less successful products than for the highly successful products (three years versus one to two years). This may indicate a loss of internal momentum during the process, or it may reflect a problem-plagued development process that dragged on without resolution.

The other important thing to note here is that each subprocess does not automatically stop when another begins; they can — and often do — overlap. For instance, concept and product testing can run concurrently with final product development. Similarly, at many companies, planning for launch starts well before final product development.

"**We believe many companies** don't give launch its due by cutting it too short and not giving the messages time to get to consumers. What is the cause of this and how can it be fixed? By selling the notion that what you need in the launch of anything is enough lead-time. You launch the public relations before the product is fixed. There's always somebody out there in the media who wants to scoop somebody else, and if the product is already in stores, there's little opportunity to write an exclusive. But if you give someone a scoop before the product is actually on shelves, then it goes from the Internet to trade magazines to general magazines."

— *Al Ries, Chairman of Ries & Ries, Atlanta, Georgia, and author of* The Fall of Advertising & the Rise of PR

When Does Launch Start?

So now we know where launch fits into the process. But what triggers its initiation? What signals that it's time to get serious about planning your new product launch? In our study, the answers varied widely. In over a third of the cases (38 percent), a product-related milestone signaled the start of launch; in these instances, having a product concept, a prototype, or an actual working product was the event that kicked off the launch phase.

Such was the case with Royal Appliance, where Jim Holcomb was involved in the highly successful launch of the original Dirt Devil vacuum cleaner in his role as vice president of marketing and strategic planning. He told us, "Launch begins once we have an operating prototype that we built in engineering. Once we decide it's a product, we go with it. That's when we start working on the launch plan, which is typically 13 to 15 months away from introduction."

For 26 percent of our survey companies, internal approvals by management, essentially the go/no-go decision, signaled the start of the launch period. Twenty-five percent of the companies said launch didn't start for them until a later point, such as when they began selling the product in the market. Consider the difference in timing between these two launch start timelines — in one, the product is a prototype, and in the other the product is on the shelf! No wonder it's difficult to understand when launch begins.

As we'll discuss in more detail in Section 5, we think it's better when the launch team arrives on the scene early enough to provide critical input into the features and design of the final product. After all, the marketing consultants are consumers as well as advertising, public relations, and promotions professionals. Having that outside voice in the room when changes can still be made might help companies avoid new product disasters.

And When Does Launch End?

As you might expect, the companies we studied all had different ideas about when the launch phase was over. More than a quarter (28 percent) said some predetermined period after being in-store marked the end of launch; 26 percent said launch ended at a specific shipping date; and almost a quarter of our sample (22 percent) used a premarket milestone such as commercialization or packaging completion to mark the conclusion of launch.

Interestingly, the companies with highly successful launches and those with less successful launches had different ideas about launch process markers. Companies with highly successful products were more likely to view the end of the launch period as a point after the product is on the shelves (35 percent), as opposed to companies with less successful product launches (25 percent). Organizations with highly successful products were nearly twice as likely as those with less successful products to consider a shipping milestone (i.e., the beginning of shipping/distribution, completion of shipping/distribution, or completion of trade marketing) as the end of launch (31 percent versus 16 percent). In contrast, companies with less successful products were twice as likely as those with highly successful products to consider a premarket milestone (i.e., the ship date or the in-store date) as the end of the launch (32 percent versus 16 percent). Interestingly, 4 percent of the companies with highly successful launches said launch was a continuous process for them, while none of the companies with less successful launches made this statement.

We always find it puzzling when companies designate the shipping date as the launch date. We realize how challenging it is to move products from R&D to manufacturing and then into the world. But the cold reality is that consumer-oriented launch activities can't begin in earnest until the product is available for purchase. We'll have much more to say in later chapters about when the launch phase should start and end. But for now, let's consider another timing issue and look at the various factors that influence the choice of a new product launch date.

Innovation Cycles Lead to Success

The survey companies said a number of key factors had either "tremendous impact" or "great impact" on the selection of a launch date. The top four factors mentioned were seasonality/cyclical considerations, chosen by 73 percent of respondents; retailer demands, named by 59 percent; sales meetings/sales force needs, which 48 percent identified as having great influence; and competitive product introductions, named by 43 percent.

Other factors that also impacted launch date timing included technology innovation, chosen by 34 percent; trade events/shows, selected by 31 percent; financial reporting, named by 30 percent; and government regulation, chosen by 9 percent.

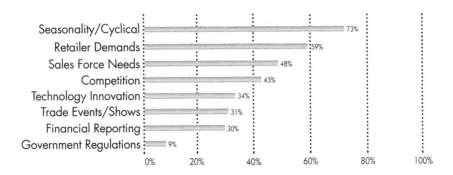

Seasonality/Cyclical — 73%
Retailer Demands — 59%
Sales Force Needs — 48%
Competition — 43%
Technology Innovation — 34%
Trade Events/Shows — 31%
Financial Reporting — 30%
Government Regulations — 9%

Factors Impacting Launch Timing

For companies included in the study, external demands seemed more likely to drive launch timing than internal, strategic concerns. We found this somewhat alarming, because rushing to meet arbitrary dates imposed by outside forces could compromise both the product and the launch campaign. The old adage that haste makes waste often proves to be true!

But once again, as we delved deeper into the data, we learned that launch timing was more likely to be driven by external factors at the companies with less successful products. For instance, 51 percent of the companies with highly successful products said sales meetings/sales force needs influenced their selection of launch dates, compared with only 40 percent of organizations with less successful products. Also, corporate financial reporting was a launch date factor for 35 percent of the highly successful products versus only 19 percent for the less successful products. Finally, cycles of technological innovation were a factor for 40 percent of the companies with highly successful products; this figure dropped to 27 percent for companies with less successful products.

The conclusion we drew from this data is that companies that innovate on a routine basis and have internal factors in place to drive innovation cycles have more successful new product launch-

> **"Clients should be** agency and communications agnostics. They should look at all their communications counsel as a brain trust and realize the best ideas can come from anywhere and not think that the only weapon in the arsenal is advertising. Consumers today don't want to be talked at; they want to discover things."
>
> — *Carol Cone, Chief Executive Officer of Cone, Inc., Boston, Massachusetts*

es. Such companies are in a better position to adequately plan and execute a new product launch. In contrast, companies that don't follow regular product launch cycles, instead allowing outside factors to determine when they'll take a new product to market, are forced into a reactive position that often results in inadequate planning for either the product or the launch ... or both.

In the next chapter, we'll investigate the planning factors that impact new product launch success.

8

GETTING

PLANNING PRIORITIES STRAIGHT

What kind of planning went into your most recent product launch? Did you write an actual launch plan? Did you start out with a plan but throw it overboard when factors (or factions) outside your control took charge and changed everything? Or did you just wing it?

If you're in the "Yep, that's us — we just winged it!" category, you're not alone. Nearly one-third of the companies (31 percent, to be exact) responding to the Schneider/Boston University New Product Launch Report said they had not created a detailed launch plan for their most recent launch.

This means a strong majority — 59 percent — of the companies did create detailed plans. Are we happy with that number? No, because if the number were higher, fewer failed products would be returned to manufacturers. Our data proves that committing a detailed plan to paper works. The companies with highly successful products were more apt to have penned a plan than those with less successful products, by a whopping margin of 72 percent to 46 percent.

Launch Strategy #2:
Have a plan

As public relations professionals, we're firmly in the camp that believes having a written plan is a key factor in launching new products successfully. We breathe easier when the plan has moved from someone's head to a piece of paper that we can hold in our hands and share with all of the launch team members. This predisposition for formal planning appears to be shared by many of our PR peers: In our study, 78 percent of the product introductions in which a PR firm was used had a physical launch document. In contrast, only 45 percent of the products introduced without a PR firm had written plans.

Now, it could be argued that if you're just launching a line extension, you don't need a full-blown launch plan. At least, that appears to be the

> **"One mistake I've seen** being made is relying on a rote formula for launch. It's not that simple any more. Believing that the traditional model of launch would hold the day in a much more complex climate doesn't work. The environment now is so complex that it's like we've gone from playing one-dimensional chess to playing three-dimensional chess. What you have now is not neatly compartmentalized any more, and you have to think more broadly. The rules have gone away, and it's more free play."
>
> — *Joe Grimaldi, Chief Executive Officer of Mullen Advertising, Wenham, Massachusetts*

thinking among the companies in our launch study. Only 6 percent of the companies whose new product introduction involved a line extension created a detailed launch plan. That number jumped to 30 percent for companies launching a category extension, and reached 55 percent for organizations launching completely new products.

What Were They Thinking?

Speaking again as firm advocates of detailed written launch plans, we're astonished that any organization would consider rolling out a completely new product without developing a comprehensive launch plan. But that's what 45 percent of the companies in our study did. We'd like to point from this statistic directly to the appalling failure rate of new products and ask, "What were you thinking?" We believe that even a line extension deserves a formal launch plan. It doesn't have to be elaborate. But for all the reasons we discussed in Section 1 about the obstacles faced by new products these days, it pays to spend time setting strategic priorities, developing creative new ways to grab consumer attention, and then committing the plan to paper.

If you don't prepare a launch plan, you'll probably fall back on the same old-same old launch strategies and tactics you've counted on in the past. But this is not a business environment that rewards hauling out the same launch plan over and over. In Section 7, we'll talk about how to keep from executing lazy launches by staying on top of launch trends and by consciously rethinking old attitudes and approaches toward launch.

What Are Your Planning Priorities?

One of the first steps in developing a launch plan is determining what your planning priorities will be. When we asked study participants where they focused their attention in the planning stage and what they considered critical to success, their answers were revealing. The differences between highly successful and less successful product launches included:

• Managers of highly successful products placed greater emphasis on brand-building efforts than did managers of less successful products. Ninety-four percent of the managers of highly successful products listed branding as either extremely critical or very important, compared with 75 percent of the managers of less successful products.

• While 82 percent of the managers of highly successful products said packaging was of high importance, only 60 percent of the managers of less successful products agreed.

• Those with highly successful products were twice as likely to pay attention to public relations during planning (33 percent) as those with less successful products (14 percent). The same was true for media coverage; 32 percent of the managers with highly successful products placed high importance on media coverage, compared with only 14 percent of other managers.

Now let's take a look at three especially interesting areas that were emphasized by managers of less successful products. First, there's trade promotion, which 51 percent of the managers of less successful products said was of high importance during their planning. In comparison, only 34 percent of the managers of highly successful products agreed that trade promotion was of high importance. Perhaps the end result was that the less successful group focused so much on trade promotion that they failed to create strategies to lure consumers into stores to see the products.

Trade advertising was also viewed slightly differently by these two groups. It was labeled highly important by 39 percent of the managers with less successful products and by 33 percent of the managers with highly successful products.

Ninety-two percent of the managers of less successful products also said distribution was highly important, a number that fell to a still impressive 84 percent among managers of highly successful products. In our experience, if you don't have distribution well organized before your launch, you don't have what it takes to win the new product wars. In the next chapter, you'll read a case study in which more forethought about the critical role of distribution during launch could have helped a company avoid an embarrassing situation that garnered unwelcome attention from *The Wall Street Journal.*

Plan Contents

The actual contents of launch plans for the products in our study tracked closely with the stated company priorities. Pricing, distribution, and positioning were included in over 90 percent of the launch plans, while financials, advertising, and sales were covered in 80 percent or more of the plans.

As you'd expect, companies that used a PR firm were more likely to have included public relations in the original plan than those who didn't, by a margin of 74 percent to 48 percent. Only 17 percent articulated an Internet strategy in their plan, a figure we're sure would be higher if we were doing the study today. But we're still surprised that *all* companies don't have a separate Internet launch plan that details how they're going to promote and sell their product on the Web. Tactics that we recommend include creating a separate "micro site" for a new product, not just listing it on the corporate site along with all of the company's other branded products. With 66 million people logging on to the Web each day,[1] consumer companies need to embrace the Internet as a powerful launch tool.

Surprisingly — and disturbingly— only 7 percent of the companies included a crisis plan as part of their launch plans. This figure should have been higher, especially since 61 percent of the companies surveyed were in the food and beverage categories, where a tainted product can be especially damaging to both the health of consumers and to a company's reputation. The vast number of things that can and do go wrong with new products is mind-boggling. Having a crisis plan at the ready enables companies to mitigate any harm to the brand if something does go wrong.

The argument we often get from launch clients about crisis plans is that the parent company has one, so the brand group doesn't need to duplicate the effort. Okay, we're happy the parent company has a plan, but how does that relate to your product? What things can go wrong with your widget? What are the messages you would convey? How would you handle a recall? An outbreak of food poisoning? Who would be the first responder? What if the corporate spokesperson weren't available? Has the corporate communications director reviewed your crisis plan? We advise putting a crisis communications plan section in every launch plan, so that if trouble strikes, you won't be scrambling to figure out how to save your brand's reputation.

> **"A lot of companies believe** you launch brands with big advertising budgets, and we say no. We say advertising has everything going for it in that you can reach the right people at the right time with the right number of messages and the messages you want, but it doesn't have credibility, and credibility is the thing that is really important for a launch."
>
> — *Al Ries, Chairman of Ries & Ries, Atlanta, Georgia, and author of* The Fall of Advertising & the Rise of PR

Delving further into plan contents, we found that the types of strategies and tactics included in launch plans were similar for both highly successful products and less successful products. This suggests that success is dictated not so much by what is covered in the plan but by the quality and execution of plan elements. In later chapters, we'll suggest ways to ensure that your plan elements are as creative and effective as possible and that all your bases are covered.

FLEXIBILITY MATTERS

Needless to say, putting your launch plan on paper doesn't guarantee everything will flow smoothly. Many things can alter the nature or course of your new product launch. That's why you need to build flexibility into your plan from the get-go.

Launch Strategy #3:
Don't Carve Your Plan in Stone

When our study participants described the events that forced them to change their launch plans, negative factors (42 percent) clearly overrode positive factors (23 percent). Product delays, competitive announcements, and regulatory problems were among the most frequent culprits. Not surprisingly, executives with highly successful products were

> **"Launching a product always** takes longer and requires more money than you can imagine. You always need more than you think."
>
> — Pete Slosberg, Founder of
> Pete's Brewing Company and
> Cocoa Pete's Chocolate Adventures,
> Campbell, California

more likely to mention positive factors than those with less successful products, by a margin of 30 percent to 10 percent. They cited outstanding retailer response, 100 percent distribution, and high consumer demand as typical positive triggers.

A vice president of marketing at a consumer technology company put it best when he told us: "Have a process, but don't be a slave to the process. In other words, be careful not to get caught. A lot of companies, big companies, have a product development life cycle and think that with launch, there's a cookie-cutter way to do it."

Interestingly, a tendency to stick to plan was more evident in highly successful launches than in less successful ones. Sixty-five percent of launches for highly successful products went extremely or very close to plan, compared with 47 percent of the less successful ones. Why? It might reflect the previously mentioned fact that highly successful launches had longer planning cycles, so they had some timing flexibility built in from the start. Or it might simply prove that these companies created better plans, anticipating what might go wrong along the launch path and making allowances for handling problems.

A Case That Cried Out for Flexibility

On January 17, 2001, Emily Nelson, a staff reporter with *The Wall Street Journal*, reported that "Kimberly-Clark expects to sell $150 million of Cottonelle Fresh Rollwipes in its first year, a goal most new products never hit."[1] The consumer products giant told Nelson that it had spent the past three years and more than $100 million on its new product, which it claimed was the first premoistened toilet paper. Kimberly-Clark filed for 30 patents on its new product. A company press spokesperson cited a one-year marketing budget of $40 million for broadcast, print, and Internet campaigns.

The story of what Kimberly-Clark promised would be "the biggest innovation in wiping technology since toilet paper rolled onto the scene more than 100 years ago" was soon showing up in media outlets like *The New York Times*, *TIME magazine*, CNN, MSNBC, and CBS News. The company bravely predicted that annual sales would reach $500 million by the product's sixth year.

Kimberly-Clark Was on a Roll, Right?

Well, not exactly. By April of 2002, Emily Nelson at *The Wall Street Journal* was again writing about the product, but in less glowing terms. This time the headline read, "Is Wet TP All Dried Up? — How One Toilet Paper Product Wiped Out After Its Launch."[2] This time, Nelson was reporting that Kimberly-Clark executives said the sales of Fresh Rollwipes were so small that they weren't "financially material."

Supermarket sales for Fresh Rollwipes during the product's first two years hit only $7.5 million. Since 50 percent of all toilet tissue sales are generated in supermarkets, all-outlet sales for the product during this time period probably amounted to maybe $15 million, or only one-tenth of what Kimberly-Clark had predicted in its publicity campaign.

What Went Wrong?

What happened between the January 2001 hype and the April 2002 bust? Plenty. The problem here could be that the American public simply wasn't ready for wet toilet paper — it was a product whose time had not yet come! And it's a perfect example of why planning and flexibility are so important in your launch plan.

Let's start with the fact that Kimberly-Clark used a national media strategy for a regional launch. The product was initially going to be available in select Southern store locations near the production plant in South Carolina. The introduction was scheduled for May but didn't actually happen until August 2001, eight full months after the national media relations campaign. Kimberly-Clark blamed the delay on manufacturing equipment that arrived late.

Okay, a major delay is one of those traumas that can happen to any launch schedule. But what's surprising is that Kimberly-Clark doesn't appear to have considered the possibility of such a delay in the product's launch plan. If they had, they probably would have altered their introductory media timetable.

But what we're more fascinated by is the decision to conduct a major national media campaign to generate demand for a product whose national availability was many, many months away. For some reason, Kimberly-Clark seems to have wanted a major new product story. Otherwise, why go public with sales predictions the likes of which are rarely heard in the packaged goods industry?

But the company's distribution strategy didn't match its media relations strategy. One important purpose of launch planning is to resolve such conflicts. In this case, though, the media strategy seems to have won out and generated interest in a product that would be available only in one part of the country later that year. By the time Fresh Rollwipes hit the shelves in the South, how many people do you think remembered what they'd heard about it?

One thing was certain: The competition was paying attention to the Fresh Rollwipes story. First, Quilted Northern introduced a product called Fresh & Moist Wipes in March 2001. By August, Procter & Gamble was selling a product called Charmin Fresh Mates Cloths in the same Southeastern markets that Fresh Rollwipes was entering. P&G had purchased patent rights to the technology to make its new product just seven weeks after Fresh Rollwipes was the story of the day across the country. The P&G product was priced at $2.99 for the starter kit with a dispenser and one roll of moist toilet paper. In contrast, a "starter pack" of Fresh Rollwipes with the special dispenser required by the moist toilet paper and four rolls had a suggested retail price of $8.99.

Four-roll refill packs of Fresh Rollwipes were priced at $3.99, or nearly $1 per roll — more than double the 45-cents-per-roll cost of regular Cottonelle toilet tissue. Is it any wonder that retailers appear to have been reluctant to stock the product? Fresh Rollwipes never rose above a 75 percent distribution rate in supermarkets (as measured by at least one unit being sold per week) in its initial launch market. In the second market where the product was introduced, the Midwest/Great Lakes region, supermarket distribution peaked at about 55 percent.

And What Else Went Wrong?

No offense to our Southeastern readers, but the fine folks in Georgia, Alabama, and Arkansas don't leap to mind when we think of avant-garde early adopters who might buy a fairly expensive, newfangled type of toilet paper. We might have chosen to go first to zip codes that have the highest numbers of bidets or consumers in cities where "new" is considered important, like New York, Los Angeles, Miami, or San Francisco.

Because Fresh Rollwipes was a product that required consumers to install a separate dispenser in their bathrooms, it would have made sense to hand out free samples so people could test the product without spending $8.99. But as Nelson reported, Kimberly-Clark failed to design Rollwipes in small trial sizes. Instead, they planned to let people test the product in a van that was scheduled to travel the Southeast during launch. Outfitted with a mobile restroom and plenty of Rollwipes, the van was going to make stops at high-traffic public events. Unfortunately, the tour was scheduled to begin in mid-September and was put on hold after the September 11 terrorist attacks.

And Finally, Let's Discuss That Campaign Strategy

We don't mean to keep picking on Kimberly-Clark, and we realize it's easy to be a Monday morning quarterback when you don't have any skin in the game. But this particular case study touches on so many of the findings from our launch study that we can't help talking about it. So let's end by discussing the theme of the campaign, which was "Wetter's Better." A $35 million TV ad campaign featured "shots of people, from behind, splashing in the water,"[3] and consumers could go on-line to read bathroom humor at www.cottonelle.com. The initial ads gave no clear explanation about the product's benefits, although more explanatory information was added as the campaign evolved.

Our question is, was this the right approach? Who was the target audience? Did they think bathroom issues were funny? Compare this with the straightforward, serious approach Pfizer took when it introduced Viagra. Pfizer made it okay to talk about the highly sensitive topic of erectile dysfunction. They used Bob Dole as their first spokesperson, before moving on to others like baseball star Raphael Palmero and NASCAR driver Mark Martin. Might not a more serious, informative approach have helped Cottonelle Fresh Rollwipes get on a roll faster?

Launch Strategy #4:
Learn to Live with the Inevitable Delays

In general, the larger the organization, the greater its love of structure. And that can include a strong desire to stay on schedule. But when it comes to new product launches, delays are almost inevitable. Seventy percent of the companies in our study reported at least one change in launch timing. Twenty percent said they had three or more timing changes; of that group, 9 percent said they had experienced four or more. That's a huge number of delays. Armed with this information, you should always consider the possibility that your launch will be delayed. What can hold you up? How can you avoid this delay? What would happen to your launch schedule if you were delayed 30 days, 60 days, or 90 days? What is your contingency plan?

On the flip side, what if your launch timetable were accelerated? What if the media broke the news of your launch before you were ready for prime time? The folks who introduced Heinz Blastin' Green Ketchup in 2000 had to cope with just that situation, in fact. Heinz was gearing up to launch a new squirt bottle after extensive research with young children, who like to draw on their food. What they planned to put into the bottle was green ketchup, but to Heinz, the main focus of the launch was going to be the fun new packaging.

A trade publication got wind of this colorful condiment and called Heinz for more information. Despite Heinz's reply that they did not plan to launch their ketchup for another six months, the editor said the news was going to appear in the publication's next issue no matter what.

Heinz had a choice to make: Do we scoop the trade pub and announce the product ourselves, or do we wait until the story breaks in the trade? Keep in mind that Heinz had planned a comprehensive launch, but now that campaign was out the window, no matter what they decided.

What would any savvy consumer products company do? They decided to retain control of this important launch. Magnet Communications, the PR firm working with Heinz on the launch, responded and within 72 hours had a plan in hand. It began with giving Associated Press the first look at the product. Video of kids using the ketchup went out to TV consumer news shows, and the only existing prototypes of the product — just six in all — were sent to the network morning shows. The result: The media went gaga over green ketchup. More than 1,000 newspapers ran the story, including *The New York Times* and *USA Today*; an estimated 198 million people were reached by the launch through TV and print.[4]

Consumers were enthralled with the notion of being able to squeeze something green onto their hot dogs and hamburgers. Heinz boosted its share of the ketchup market from 50 percent to 56 percent in the 12 months after launching its Blastin' Green ketchup. The launch was so successful that Heinz followed up the green condiment with Funky Purple, Stellar Blue, and even a Mystery Color, a limited edition version that sold out in just eight weeks. Each new color upped Heinz's market share, and by the end of 2002, they owned 60 percent of the ketchup market.[5]

As you can see from the Heinz example, sticking to the original launch schedule does not appear to be a driving success factor. And in fact, there were no differences between highly successful and less successful projects on this measure.

Where a real difference emerged was in the managers' attitudes toward change. The study findings suggest that companies that were more flexible about launch timing achieved the best results. Nearly half (48 percent) of the executives involved in highly successful launches said it was important to be flexible about launch timing, but only 26 percent of the executives whose launches were less successful agreed that timing should be flexible. Imagine the frustration that undoubtedly overtakes the 74 percent of people with less successful launches who believe that timing should not be flexible. This is where being inflexible can really hurt.

Based on the results of our study, we recommend that launch teams learn to not just expect delays but to live with them as well. A launch timetable so rigid that it offers no way to adjust to good or bad events is in serious trouble from day one.

Take the time to think and plan for various contingencies. Create a list of all the good things that could happen: tons of media coverage, incredible consumer demand, a celebrity embracing your product and hyping it on his/her program, the president being photographed using your product. Then make a list of all the negative things that could happen: the product not being shipped on time, the product arriving at the retailer after the commercials begin running, the product being recalled because it's defective, a competitor introducing a cheaper but similar product with better shelf placement.

Finally, consider developing a layered launch plan that allows for the possibility of the unexpected. Using a multilayered approach will enable you to be prepared for unplanned events that may temporarily derail your launch plan.

SELECTING NEW PRODUCTS AND THE TEAM

The Schneider/Boston University New Product Launch Report uncovered some interesting information about several characteristics that help new products succeed. We also learned who should be on the launch team and which team members make the best leaders. In this section, we'll look at the launch success factors that emerged in each of these areas.

10

GIVE CONSUMERS
SOMETHING REALLY NEW

In **Section 1, we talked about** five categories of new products: brand positioning
products, brand extensions, line extensions,
products that are new to the company, and
products that are totally new to the world. In
our study, we found that products that fit into
these last two categories have the greatest
chance of success.

But only 14 percent of the companies we studied had introduced a new product that featured
a major technological break-
through. Among the highly
successful products, 20 percent were based on technological breakthroughs, while only
5 percent of the less successful
products fit this description.

In addition, highly successful products were much more
likely than less successful
ones to fit the "new to the

> **"When you've got a new consumer**
> product and it's a technology product,
> you cannot launch a product; you have
> to launch a lifestyle. Launch the product
> in the context of the consumer's lifestyle.
> Show why it is relevant to the
> consumer's life."
>
> — *Hector Marinez, Vice President of*
> *Porter Novelli Bay Area, San Francisco,*
> *California*

company" classification, by a margin of 63 percent to 46 percent. Study participants defined "newness" broadly; they included not just technology and uniqueness but innovations in packaging, advertising, and distribution.

Launch Strategy #5:
Spend Money on Products That Are "New"

What do these findings suggest? We all know that consumers crave newness (as do the reporters who follow consumer products), so it's possible that products involving technological breakthroughs were destined for higher success rates no matter how their launches had been handled. But even though we're strong proponents of breakthrough innovation, we don't subscribe to the build-it-and-they-will-come philosophy. The fact is, many new technologies flop. Some are too complicated or too expensive, or they're first versions that don't perform well because they were rushed to market. Other breakthrough bombs are ideas that are too far ahead of their time. Finally, some innovations just don't appeal to enough people to justify their development and marketing costs.

More Resources = More Success

For all these reasons and more, you can see that putting out a breakthrough product doesn't guarantee commercial success. We believe, in fact, that the higher success rate we saw among breakthrough products in our study was at least partly because of the greater resources devoted to these truly new products.

Real innovation is costly, so companies generally have more riding on breakthrough products than on line extensions. With substantial human resources and higher budget allocations, it's not surprising that breakthrough products have a better chance of launch success than less exciting products that don't receive the same level of support. We'll talk more in Chapter 12 about how larger launch budgets can greatly boost your success rate.

The Line Extension Challenge

A total of 12 percent of the products in our study were categorized as line extensions, with 8 percent in the less successful group and 4 percent in the highly successful group. This difference in success rates highlights the fact that not all line extensions are created equal.

"High-value line extensions offer consumers a new and important benefit and can contribute just as much incremental growth to the parent brand, manufacturer, or category as a totally new brand," said IRI's Valerie Skala. "Adding sun protection to a facial moisturizer is a good example of a high-value line extension. The product now attracts people who are concerned about the aging effects of the sun or about skin cancer but who had not previously used a daily facial moisturizer because they didn't have dry skin and didn't feel they needed it.

"Another example is when the household cleaning manufacturers introduced premoistened pads for wet mopping that work on the same mop handle originally introduced for dry dust mopping. In each of these cases, they brought a whole new benefit to the consumer."

The other type of line extension is the me-too product that merely matches a competitor's offering without adding anything new or different in any significant way. The consumer product landscape, in fact, is littered with this type of offering.

There are certainly logical reasons for launching me-too products. When Brand X introduces a new feature or benefit, for example, competing brands often will rush to add it to their own lines so buyers won't have any reason to switch to Brand X.

Another reason for the large number of me-too line extensions is that it's fairly common practice for the number two or three player in a category to take the position of "fast follower." The category leader takes the risk and invests in consumer research and education, while the fast follower focuses resources on quickly identifying and imitating the leader's hot new products, accepting a lower reward in exchange for lower risk. (The "order of entry" statistics show that sales of the second entrant into a new product segment are usually well below those of the first entrant.)

Yet another reason for me-too line extensions is that it's not uncommon for more than one manufacturer to recognize, say, a new flavor or scent trend, and for all of them to end up launching similar products within months of one another, each thinking they'll be first to market.

Still, empirical evidence indicates that many manufacturers are practicing the we-have-to-introduce-something-new strategy beyond the point of diminishing returns, even spending money to launch products that are not payback propositions. They get caught in the trap of "escalation bias": New product initiatives advance to launch with no strong "gates" in place that force the team to pause and reevaluate whether the initiative still has a strong likelihood of paying out. Research has shown that the companies that are most successful with new products have defined hurdles at several stages of the new product development cycle, and projects that don't clear those hurdles are killed or held back for further development.

Take laundry detergent, for example. Nearly every consumer already uses laundry detergent, so category growth isn't going to be significant. And if you're already a big player in the laundry detergent category, growing your share of this heavily saturated market is tough. Absent a major breakthrough in either washing machines or detergent technology, your options are limited to manufacturing cost reductions that increase profitability; minor line extensions, such as a new scent; and value-added line extensions that boost dollar (though not unit) sales and perhaps steal market share from a competitor.

Yes, in some categories, like ice cream and snacks, a regular infusion of new flavors is needed to keep consumers' taste buds tingling. And sometimes you have to bring out a line extension just to defend your category leadership. But in most situations, IRI's Skala advises, a more effective path to growth is to keep looking for high-value line extensions and for new products that capture consumers you're not already reaching.

"If you're in the carbonated soft drinks business, for example, you might look at 'liquid refreshment' purchase and usage occasions when consumers are not choosing your category, analyze the different need-states, and see what you could offer them," Skala said. "You can expand the range of offerings within your category through new product formulations, flavors, or package types. Or you expand into new categories, such as noncarbonated fruit drinks, bottled water, and sports drinks. Or you pioneer totally new categories like flavor- and nutrient-enhanced water."

Internal Impact of Line Extensions

Another rationale for focusing on new products or high-value line extensions instead of sticking with me-too line extensions is the different ways these two strategies will impact your company internally. It's easy to justify devoting substantial marketing resources and energy to breakthrough products or line extensions that offer consumers real benefits, but it's difficult to drum up internal enthusiasm for yet another copycat line extension.

Of course, since a company has less riding on a me-too line extension's success, it's easier to tolerate lackluster results. After all, development and marketing costs are negligible, and distribution is already in place. And if the line extension provides incremental income at relatively low cost, who's going to complain?

But beware: Relying on an endless string of line extensions not only lulls your marketing department to sleep, it also poses other serious dangers. While the organization is focusing on iterative line extensions, they may not recognize in time that the marketplace is shifting in a new direction. A *New York Times* article in October 2003 discussed how Kraft Foods had taken the Oreo cookie to new sales heights through aggressive line extensions: colored crème filling for holidays, chocolate crème filling, two-flavor filling, mini-size cookies, and so on. The marketing experts quoted in the article warned that "too much tinkering could tarnish the brand."[1] But the bigger danger we saw is that, as the article points out, cookie sales are slowing as Americans change their eating habits to reflect healthier choices. Various consumer and advocacy groups are demanding the removal of fat, sugar, and carbohydrates from snack foods and encouraging lower consumption of these foods in general. How much time will it take the research and development team to switch gears from flavor/color/size variations to significant product formulation changes?

What we'd like to emphasize here is that perhaps it makes more sense to focus on totally new products and high-value line extensions rather than pouring resources into ho-hum line extensions that support the status quo. You need to make sure you're anticipating the future direction of your market, not just clinging to your comfort zone, no matter how profitable that may have been in the past. Keep in mind the demographic and behavioral trends we discussed in Section 1, including the rapid aging and ethnic changes in the population. Consider what impact those changes will have on consumer demand for your current products. Will a stream of copycat line extensions enable your company to succeed in this changing marketplace, or do you need products that reflect bold new thinking?

A Portfolio Approach

The key to understanding the benefits of innovative new products versus minor line extensions lies in using a portfolio approach, as espoused by our colleague and innovation guru Mark Sebell in his book *Ban the Humorous Bazooka [and Avoid Roadblocks and Speed Bumps along the Innovation Highway]*. Sebell describes three levels of innovation: incremental (i.e., line extensions); breakthrough, which produces a meaningful change in the way you do business to give consumers something demonstrably new; and transformational, which usually involves introducing a technology that creates a new industry or transforms the way we work.[2] Sebell recommends investing resources into each of these areas rather than focusing entirely on just one. Instead of adding only line extensions, consider giving consumers something totally different than what they expect from your company. This way, you lower the chance of a competitor overtaking you by creating a whole new market segment that you hadn't even dreamed of developing.

In fact, the degree of innovation in your new product will have substantial implications for your launch strategy, as illustrated in the Product Innovation Spectrum below.

PRODUCT INNOVATION SPECTRUM

Revolutionary Product	Evolutionary Product	Line Extension
Product is king! Celebrate!	Product still reigns; begin borrowed interest	Insert into stakeholder lifestyle

Building Brand Voice

- Product attributes
- Engineering/R&D
- Early adopters

- Spokespeople
- Testimonials/Third party
- Sponsorships

- Broader context - societal issues & trends
- Cause marketing
- Celebrities

As the graphic indicates, the launch message and brand voice change as a product moves across the innovation spectrum:

- **REVOLUTIONARY PRODUCT:** When you launch a breakthrough product, you can ballyhoo its attributes and herald its challenging development. During this stage, early adaptors make good messengers because they often become almost evangelical in their zeal to tell others about the great new product they've found. Cultivating these "apostles" is essential so they can create buzz and set the stage for others to consider your product's merits; these individuals are the ticket to your product's future.

- **EVOLUTIONARY PRODUCT:** At this stage, you've still got a solid product with strong benefits, but it's no longer a totally new idea. At the revolutionary stage, all you needed to talk about was your product because it was so new, different, and exciting. With an evolutionary product, you need to determine how and where the product fits into the outside world, and then borrow some interest from that world to continue creating excitement about your product. This often involves bringing on board third-party spokespeople who can lend their credibility to your message. You may also want to use sponsorships and similar marketing opportunities to spread your launch message to a more broad-based audience.

- **LINE EXTENSION PRODUCT:** Now you've built a customer base, and you want to make sure they continue to embrace your product as part of their lifestyle. At this point, line extensions are imperative to keep your product in the consumer consciousness. To break through the clutter, you'll need to create a strong lifestyle message that shows how your product fits into the broader context of societal issues and trends. Celebrities and cause-related marketing can be useful vehicles because they lend credibility, excitement, and emotional aspects to your launch.

One of the challenges of constantly working at the line extension end of the Product Innovation Spectrum is keeping your launch team energized. An endless stream of line extensions can produce a ho-hum attitude that fights against, rather than boosts, team member creativity.

Interestingly, some of the strategies that are most effective with line extension launches, such as celebrity involvement and cause-related marketing, can reignite the launch team's interest for the same reasons that they resonate with consumers. The excitement of working with a celebrity or the passion that a campaign engenders when it benefits a worthy cause can pay dividends for your team too.

Placing the line extension in the context of larger societal issues and trends can also help keep team interest alive. People like to believe their work is part of a bigger world. That's why it's important to make sure team members recognize where a new product fits in the context of consumers' lives, instead of just where it fits within the company's business context. By constantly looking outward as well as inward, the team can be encouraged to make linkages with the external world that will help improve the launch.

On-Shelf Presence Is Key

Let's look at another product-related finding of our study. Our participants reported a wide spectrum of introductory SKUs, from one to more than 50. Nonetheless, the division between highly successful launches and less successful launches shows that more SKUs are definitely better.

Thirty-four percent of highly successful products rolled out with more than 10 SKUs, compared with just 15 percent of the less successful efforts. Sixty-one percent of the less successful products had only one to four SKUs. Consumers like choice — so give it to them.

These findings reinforce the importance of an on-shelf/in-store presence to product success. It's Marketing 101 all over again: You need shelf presence to get consumers' attention, and you need the trade's attention to command shelf space. As we discussed in Chapter 5, the prevalence of slotting fees has made achieving on-shelf presence more challenging, but our study results show that product placement on the shelf is vital to success.

Now, let's look at another issue that is equally critical to launch success: the composition of your launch team.

11

TEAMS WORK

The people who travel with you on your launch journey are extremely important. In our research, team formation and composition (both internal and external) emerged as critical launch success factors. The key study findings here are that teams are good, big teams are better, and multidisciplinary teams work best. In addition, the earlier your team comes together, the better your chances of success.

Launch Strategy #6:
Assemble an Expert Launch Crew

Launch teams were established in 60 percent of the new product launches we studied, and the highly successful products were more likely to be managed by a team (69 percent) than the less successful ones (54 percent).

An analysis of team composition revealed these interesting results:

• The typical team includes at least one marketing vice president/marketing manager/brand manager. This was true for 90 percent of the companies in our study.

• For those instances in which a marketing vice president/marketing manager/brand manager is not on the team, the team is most apt to be managed by the chief executive officer and to include just one or two other people.

• One or more people from operations/engineering, manufacturing, or product development/R&D are also usually present. This was true 81 percent of the time in our study group.

• Communications and information technology are included as core members only on very large teams (10-plus members).

Team Size Makes a Difference

Bringing more brainpower to launch planning made a significant difference in the launch's success. On average, the launch teams included five or six core members, but team size varied considerably between the highly successful product launches and the less successful ones. Here are the key findings:

• The teams that launched highly successful products were far more likely to include six or more people than the teams that launched less successful products. Among the teams supporting highly successful products, 38 percent had six to seven members and 22 percent had eight or more members. This means a total of 60 percent of these teams had six or more members. In contrast, only 34 percent of the teams for the less successful products had six or more participants.

• Teams of five or fewer people supported 67 percent of the less successful launches. In contrast, only 40 percent of the highly successful products had teams of five or fewer people.

• The percentage of launch teams with only one to three people was almost three times higher among less successful products than among the highly successful products. Twenty-nine percent of the teams for less successful products included just one to three people, while only 10 percent of the highly successful products had teams this small.

The bottom line: Be inclusive when you form your launch team.

It may be harder to manage a larger team, but rest assured, in the end it will pay off.

Who Should Sit Around the Table

Clearly, size matters when forming your launch team. With more seats at the table, you can bring together a truly integrated team with all the skills and experience needed to create and implement a winning launch plan.

The membership makeup of the core launch team was one area where the results of quantitative research differed significantly from our qualitative information. First, let's look at the results of the quantitative research.

- External agencies, such as public relations and advertising, were typically not part of the core launch teams. Just 25 percent of the executives surveyed reported including external suppliers or support groups as members of their core teams. Seventy-six percent, however, used external groups as secondary team members.

> **"Some of the best launches** I've worked on involved bringing in a team of all the disciplines and working together on developing the plan and implementation. Stretch the integration of the team beyond marketing to include people from other parts of the client organization. For example, for the Mohegan Sun launch, we met on a regular basis with the communications people, the people who ran the casino, the security staff, and the people who ran the hospitality portions of the facility. We were updated on what stage we were at in implementing our parts of the plan and we generated ideas. One of the biggest PR boosts we got was when the woman who was training people to be craps dealers told us about her work. We realized how cool it would be to have reporters come in and learn how to do these jobs. It produced a phenomenal volume of PR in the months before the opening, including coverage from feature writers who are hard to get. We might never have thought of that idea unless the launch team had been broadly integrated."
>
> *— Tom Bradley, Vice President and Director of PR for Mintz & Hoke, Avon, Connecticut*

- Advertising agencies had the greatest team presence overall; 69 percent of the teams included the advertising agency as either a core or a secondary member. A sizeable minority also included package design firms (40 percent), public relations firms (33 percent), and promotions firms (24 percent) on their core secondary teams.

This chart illustrates the typical makeup of the core and secondary launch teams:

TRADITIONAL LAUNCH TEAM COMPOSITION

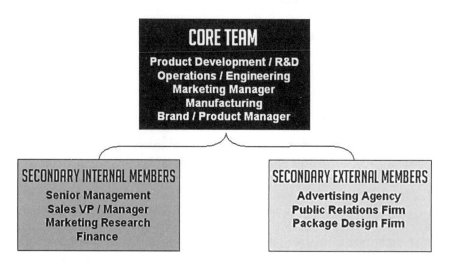

CORE TEAM

Product Development / R&D
Operations / Engineering
Marketing Manager
Manufacturing
Brand / Product Manager

SECONDARY INTERNAL MEMBERS

Senior Management
Sales VP / Manager
Marketing Research
Finance

SECONDARY EXTERNAL MEMBERS

Advertising Agency
Public Relations Firm
Package Design Firm

These results stand in stark contrast to the qualitative research phase, where all companies surveyed reported having external agency members on their core launch teams. As you'll recall, all 10 executives in this phase of the study were award-winning launch experts, so we should probably pay attention to the fact that all of them included their ad, PR, and promotions agencies on their core launch teams. Also, with the Internet now a major force in channel distribution, Web developers and other Internet partners should be included on the core team as well.

We developed the following diagram to illustrate a proposed methodology for creating launch teams. The core launch team members (marketing, operations, and sales) anchor the launch process, with the external agencies available as resources for the core team from day one of planning. All participants also need to interact with senior management from time to time throughout the launch process for approvals and funding.

Creating a core team that is truly integrated ensures that all messages, themes, and implementation plans are coordinated. Also, the earlier you bring your launch team together, the better. By getting an early start, they can begin to work effectively as a group to create powerful results.

PROPOSED LAUNCH TEAM COMPOSITION

Subway Takes Team Integration to the Nth Degree

It's always rewarding when clients allow agencies to practice what they preach. When Subway asked Schneider & Associates to help craft a childhood obesity prevention program, the first thing we proposed to Chris Carroll, senior vice president-director of marketing at Subway, was to hold a strategic planning session with all the players who were working on the obesity issue.

We needed a big room to accomplish this goal because we ended up including 25 people. In addition to the Schneider team, participants included Subway's advertising and media buying agencies, a kids marketing firm, and internal Subway staff from research, finance, kids marketing, promotions, advertising, and communications. In short, it was the integrated marketing dream team. To set the stage, a nutrition expert and author from a major university provided an overview of the obesity problem in the United States. Next came a presentation by three specialists in kids marketing, who described the tween and teen market. This was followed by Subway's ad agency, which showed the group a flight of commercials produced by and featuring teens reinforcing Subway's "healthy choice" message. Finally, Chris Carroll briefly reviewed the importance of dealing with childhood obesity as a QSR (Quick Service Restaurant).

Our professional facilitator used this information to moderate an ideation session. Having an outside facilitator trained in running creative sessions allowed all the internal and agency people to just sit back and generate great ideas. The beauty of this integrated group was that each person in the room had his or her unique perspective on what would impact children. The group generated hundreds of ideas, and the result was a new children's program with the working title "Kids Eat Fresh."

The goal of the team meeting was to develop a campaign that could be supported through media relations, advertising, sales promotion, the Internet, and point of sale. Looking back, it's amazing how many of the "wishes" we articulated for the campaign have come true. We wanted to:

Be sure the Subway Kids' Pak™ was healthy

Subway beefed up the Kids' Pak's nutritional content by redesigning it to include a fresh deli-style sandwich, a Minute Maid 100 percent fruit juice box, and a General Mills Fruit Roll-Up fruit snack. In addition to the nutritional changes, the Kids' Pak added an activity-inspired toy to encourage physical exercise and play. The toys included a flying disk, golf club, kite, football, and rattle.

Conduct primary research to determine kids' perceptions of healthy eating

Subway conducted primary research through a children's research company called Tucker, Draddy, Kane and Partners. The project included talking with moms and kids ages five to 10.

Involve Jared Fogle

Subway's weight-loss hero and brand spokesperson was an over-weight child who grew up to be an obese adult and then changed his life through diet and exercise.

Fogle is a natural fit as the spokesperson for Subway's Childhood Obesity Prevention Program. His personal experience as an overweight child, teenager, and adult is a story that people of all ages continue to relate to. As part of Fogle's role, Subway developed the "Jared & Friends School Tour," a national campaign where Jared Fogle or his other weight-loss "friends" would travel to elementary schools across the country to share their stories of weight-loss success and educate kids about smart eating choices and regular exercise. Fogle kicked off the campaign at the Anna Silver School for Arts and Technology in New York City and continues to travel around the country talking to kids in schools about the importance of making healthy choices and exercising. As of March 2004, Fogle had visited more than 30,000 students across the country.

Involve athletes in this direct-to-kids program

Basketball player Lisa Leslie from the WNBA Los Angeles Sparks, and Olympic gold medallist, joined Fogle in educating young people about the importance of healthy eating and regular exercise. Leslie participated in the New York City campaign kickoff and continues to communicate Subway's message to moms and children. As an athlete, Leslie is an authority on sports and exercise and was able to enhance Fogle's messaging about weight loss and food choices.

Communicate directly with kids on-line

Kids can learn about health and nutrition through fun, interactive games at www.subwaykids.com. Subway developed the Internet site specifically to engage kids in a fun yet educational way. Children are accessing a vast majority of their information on-line, and it was integral to have a place where kids could interact with the brand. Interactive games such as "The

Healthilizer," "Battle of the Burger Droids," "Wrassle-Rama," and "Build-a-Power-Meal" give parents and their children the chance to learn about the benefits of a good diet and exercise regimen in a lighthearted manner. In addition, Subway created a Web site for parents that links to www.subwaykids.com. Entitled "Subway Steps to Healthier Kids," it focuses on a healthy diet and active lifestyle and serves as a resource for parents striving to manage their children's diet and exercise levels.

Have a grassroots, educational program at grade school level to educate kids about healthy eating

In partnership with *Weekly Reader*, the largest and oldest educational magazine for students, Subway developed an in-school curriculum entitled "One Body! One Life! Eat Fresh! Get Fit." Featuring Jared Fogle and Lisa Leslie, the curriculum is being distributed to fourth, fifth, and sixth graders in more than 60,000 schools. More than 10 million kids aged nine to 12 will learn about proper eating and exercise choices through educational quizzes and activities. Students also receive a food and exercise tracker to help them monitor their eating and exercise habits to make healthier choices.

Have third-party influencers (psychologists, nutritionists, physicians) advise us in the campaign to make sure we were being true to our mission

Experts like Dr. Kelly Brownell of Yale University, author of *Food Fight*, and Dr. Walter Willett, Harvard University's world-renowned nutritionist, are frequently consulted by the media about childhood obesity prevention. Schneider & Associates distributes regular key influencer mailings to these experts and other key influencers in the health, nutrition, and education communities to continually educate them on Subway's efforts to provide healthy choices for kids.

Who Sits in the Big Chair?

The person who ultimately controls your launch plays a critical role in its success. Once again, our study revealed interesting differences between who led the charge in highly successful launch-es versus who headed the less successful ones. Depending on your position in the organization, you may or may not have a vote on who is going to lead the team. But our study arms you with some empirical evidence about who makes the best launch leader and why.

Let's look first at the overall findings about team leaders and then talk about the differences we found between highly successful and less successful products:

- Overall, marketing vice presidents and marketing directors were most likely to have primary responsibility for the product introduction; people in these positions headed 37 percent of the launches in our study.

- Brand, product, or new product managers led nearly one-quarter (24 percent) of the introductions.

- Marketing managers conducted 14 percent of the launches, and other senior management representatives led 13 percent.

When we looked for differences in team leadership between the highly successful products and the less successful ones, here are the comparative success rates we discovered within the three groups of potential team leaders:

Brand/Product Manager

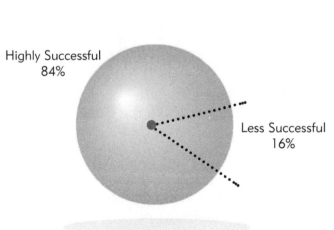

Highly Successful
84%

Less Successful
16%

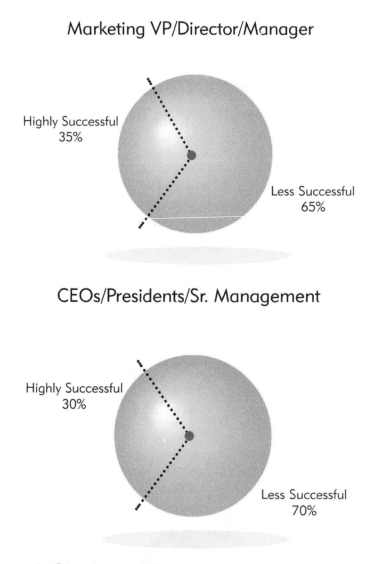

Marketing VP/Director/Manager

Highly Successful
35%

Less Successful
65%

CEOs/Presidents/Sr. Management

Highly Successful
30%

Less Successful
70%

Launch Strategy #7:
Brand/Product Managers Make the Best Team Leaders

Clearly, empowering a brand manager or a new product manager to sit at the head of the table pays dividends. Their launch success rate far outdistances those of other team leader titles — probably because good brand and product managers live the product every day and know how to get things done.

A successful product introduction requires a leader who is totally dedicated to the task of launching his or her new product, without other responsibilities or distractions. Compare the single-minded focus of a product manager with the daily juggling act that is the lot of chief executive officers and presidents. Once you realize how much focus is required to bring a product to market, it's easy to understand why company leaders are not the best people to captain launch teams.

Marketing guru Al Ries believes there's another factor at work here too: "I've met with CEOs who have no experience at all in marketing, and I give them an idea and they say, 'No, that's not right.' They wouldn't go to their doctor or lawyer and do that, but they'll do that to their marketing people. The problem lies with the widespread misconception that marketing is common sense, so anybody can do it and there probably isn't any particular advantage to studying marketing."

While Ries doesn't believe this misunderstanding is going to go away anytime soon, that doesn't mean company leaders shouldn't participate in launch efforts. Their visible enthusiasm for the new product and the strategy devised to introduce it is essential for generating the widespread internal and financial support that a successful launch needs. Team members have to know that the ultimate decision maker is on board this fast-moving launch train; otherwise, they can end up struggling for resources.

Speaking of resources, in the next section we'll reveal what we learned about budgets and share the final three launch success strategies that emerged from our study.

PUT YOUR MONEY WHERE
IT COUNTS MOST

The odds of a product remaining on the shelf for more than a year depend partly on the marketing support it receives during its introductory period. We wish we could report the discovery of a magical budget formula for new product launches, but unfortunately it's not that easy. What we did learn is that where you spend your money makes a big difference in your chances for success. In this section we offer key guidelines for getting the most impact for your dollars.

12

BREAKING DOWN THE LAUNCH BUDGET

A **successful launch requires** investment. It's no surprise that the most effective launches in our study were backed by substantially larger budgets than the less successful ones. But what we learned about *where* the successful launch teams spent their money can help you make better decisions about your own budget.

Launch Strategy # 8:
Bigger Budgets Fuel Success

The average one-year budget for the highly successful products in our study was $4.7 million, which is 88 percent higher than the average budget of $2.5 million for the less successful products. One caveat: Interpret these

"**Assuming that you have** to spend a lot of money is a mistake. We specialize in doing a lot without a big budget; to me the preferred thing is to do something without any executables — getting gossip column items and crazy stuff. They're low risk. If it sticks, it's great. If not, what did you invest in it?"

— *Sal Cataldi, President and Creative Director of Cataldi PR, New York, New York* numbers with a little caution because we included a wide range of launch types (national rollouts, regional rollouts, test markets) in the study sample. But even allowing for those differences, it's clear that bigger budgets are better:

- Overall, the average year one marketing budget was $3.7 million.[1] Almost six in 10 products (58 percent) had first-year budgets of less than $1 million, while 13 percent reported budgets of over $10 million. Six percent reported budgets of over $20 million.

- The launch budgets varied by product category. Food and beverage products had the highest average budget of $4.6 million, followed by apparel and shoes with $3.3 million, sporting goods with $0.8 million, and health and beauty with $0.3 million.

- The average budget for a national introduction was $5 million, while national phased rollouts used an average budget of $3.9 million. Regional introductions had an average budget of $2 million, but the test market budget average was much lower at only $300,000.

While only 6 percent of the marketers in the study had budgets greater than $20 million, our research on launch budgets since the study's completion indicates that higher price tags are not unusual. For example, in preparation for the Schneider & Associates 2003 Most Memorable New Product Launch Survey, we chronicled some of the budgets for launches executed in 2003. The U.S. Bureau of Engraving  & Printing invested $33 million in the new $20 bill to educate consumers, retailers, and banks about the benefits of the revamped currency. The Procter & Gamble Co., meanwhile, spent $50 to $75 million launching Crest® Night Effects™. And with Food and Drug Administration approval of Claritin® OTC, Schering-Plough Corp. pumped an estimated $40 million into advertising and public relations to reach consumers.

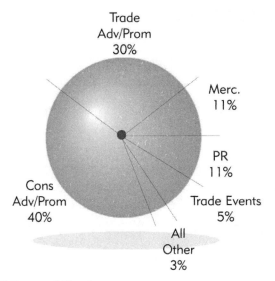

Trade
Adv/Prom
30%

Merc.
11%

PR
11%

Trade Events
5%

All
Other
3%

Cons
Adv/Prom
40%

Where the Money Went

As we've already hinted, our research suggests that when it comes to launch budgets, it's not just how much money you have, but how you spend it. The following chart shows where study participants, on average, spent their launch budgets for a range of marketing support activities.

The activities that usually garnered the greatest slice of the marketing pie were consumer advertising/promotions, which accounted for an average 40 percent of first-year budgets, and trade advertising/promotions (including slotting), which accounted for an average 30 percent of first-year budgets. Of course, these allocations varied from product category to product category. Health and beauty products adopted a substantially stronger consumer focus, with an average 55 percent of first-year budgets allocated to consumer advertising and promotions and only 10 percent going to trade advertising and promotions. In contrast, the apparel and shoes category directed its energies more toward the trade, with 52 percent of launch budgets going in this direction, compared with only 32 percent going to consumer-targeted efforts.

A closer analysis of the marketing budget allocations revealed four distinct strategies for budget allocation:

- **CONSUMER-FOCUSED:** spent 78 percent of marketing dollars on consumer-related activities

- **TRADE-FOCUSED:** devoted 86 percent of funds to trade-related support

- **CONSUMER/TRADE:** split budgets roughly evenly between consumer (47 percent) and trade (42 percent) efforts

- **DIVERSE:** spread marketing funds across a wide range of support activities, with no one area receiving more than 30 percent of the budget

The Consumer/Trade and Consumer-focused segments maintained the largest average marketing budgets at $10.8 million and $3.9 million, respectively. Interestingly, the Diverse segment used a generally lower average budget of $1.6 million, suggesting that less money was being spread across a wide range of support activities.

Pull Strategy Outperforms Push Strategy

An important finding emerged when we looked at which strategies had been used for highly successful launches and which were employed in less successful launches. Here we discovered that strategies focusing on trade initiatives were less successful than those geared primarily toward consumers. In other words, adopting a "push" strategy for launch that says "put it on the shelf and they will come" is far less effective than using a "pull" strategy that drives consumers into stores seeking your new product.

Launch Strategy #9:
Consumer-focused Spending Prevents Crash Landings

The largest segment of the highly successful products, 35 percent, used the Consumer-focused strategy, compared with 22 percent of the less successful products. In contrast, the less successful products were more likely to favor the Trade-focused strategy (25 percent) or the Diverse strategy (28 percent). Among the highly successful products, only 14 percent took the Trade-focused route, and 18 percent used the Diverse strategy.

Even though combined Consumer/Trade budgets were almost three times as high as straight consumer spending budgets, it appears that marketing dollars focused directly on the consumer are more effective than dollars split for Consumer/Trade strategies. Managers who put money into Consumer/Trade strategies were just as likely to fail as they were to succeed; of the companies that used this strategy, 18 percent had highly successful products and 16 percent ended up with less successful products.

When we asked the survey participants for their opinions on where they got the most bang for their bucks, their perceptions reinforced our conclusion that programs geared directly to consumers enhanced the chance of launch success. Activities with the greatest perceived return on investment were consumer oriented: consumer advertising (51 percent), consumer promotions (44 percent), and merchandising (43 percent).

All of these techniques help you get into a conversation with consumers, a critical step in a society where word-of-mouth advertising is the best advertising you can have. The authors of *The Influentials*, Jon Berry and Ed Keller, put it this way: "When Americans make decisions today, it's a conversation. Before Americans buy, they talk. And they listen. The first step in the buying process is to ask a friend, family member, or the expert close at hand what *they* think."[2]

> **"There is a strange belief** out there that because media relations is 'free,' that $250,000 or $300,000 is enough for a national launch. Purchased media and events should support the media relations launch. You need to have the right sort of budget to seed the market at the grassroots level. Getting into people's minds — that's critical and expensive."
>
> — *Carol Cone, Chief Executive Officer of Cone, Inc., Boston, Massachusetts*

Launch Strategy #10:
Don't Overlook PR

In their best-selling book, *The Fall of Advertising & the Rise of PR*, Al Ries and Laura Ries give example after example of new products and brands that have relied heavily — and in some instances solely — on public relations to gain the early consumer attention needed for a successful launch. They make a strong case that public relations is the most effective tool for launching new brands and products, while advertising should be used to sustain consumer interest over time.

Our study revealed that these lessons are not yet fully understood in the new product community, where PR continues to be an underutilized weapon in the launch arsenal. Furthermore, our numbers showed that public relations' positive impact was extremely significant for highly successful products. Overall, in fact, PR was perceived as being best at building awareness among consumers and the trade by generating excitement for a product.

But just 44 percent of the new product cases in our study included a PR firm's assistance for the most recent product launches. Less than 60 percent of the companies that employed a PR firm included PR on the core team for the product introduction. Virtually all of those organizations, however, used an advertising agency on the core launch team.

We also found that highly successful products were much more likely to engage in PR-related activities than less successful ones. While 76 percent of the highly successful products engaged a PR firm to help plan and execute launch, less than 60 percent of less successful ones did the same.

The Link between PR and Launch Savvy

Interestingly, the strategic use of public relations appears to be a lead indicator of launch know-how overall. The companies in the study that used a PR firm tended to match up with some of our chief launch success factors far better than the companies that did not use outside PR support. Companies that used a PR firm were:

• More likely to be introducing an entirely new product. Sixty-eight percent of the companies using a PR firm were launching truly new products. Among the companies that did not use a PR firm, only 45 percent were launching a totally new product.

• More apt to be capitalizing on a major technological breakthrough in product development. Seventy-five percent of the companies employing a PR firm fell into this category, compared with just 25 percent of the firms that did not use a PR agency.

• More likely to have formulated a launch plan. Seventy-eight percent of the companies that used a PR firm had written launch plans, compared with 45 percent of the companies that did not use a PR firm.

• Committed to putting more total funds into the introductory marketing effort. Marketing budgets for companies that used a PR firm averaged 48 percent higher ($5.2 million) than companies without external PR support ($2.5 million).

We asked companies that used a public relations firm for their most recent product introduction to evaluate the impact of both marketing and public relations activities on product launch success. Executives with highly successful launches reported significantly greater returns and perceived impact across all public relations-related activities. The average impact rating across all PR activities was 76 percent for highly successful products, compared with 56 percent for less successful ones. This suggests that more comprehensive PR programs are likely to provide greater impact in the marketplace. Overall, the public relations activities perceived as having the greatest impact were those likely to build awareness among the media, consumers, and the trade by generating excitement about the product.

> **"Some people are paying** big bucks for Super Bowl ads, but they don't leverage it with PR. If you've already spent the big dollars on the ads, then take soft dollars and put it into PR to promote that XYZ Company is doing the ad. Most sponsors at that level are ignoring this, but if they thought it through, they might be able to find a reason to tie in with PR. You could put another quarter of a million dollars in the budget for PR and get that much more bang for your original $2 million investment in a Super Bowl ad."
>
> — *Alan Taylor, Chief Executive Officer of Alan Taylor Communications, New York, New York*

We've now introduced you to all 10 of the launch lessons that emerged in the Schneider/Boston University New Product Launch Report. So enough with all the statistics! In the coming sections you'll learn how to leverage these strategies to ensure that your next new product launch reaches unparalleled heights of success!

STARTING THE COUNTDOWN
TO LAUNCH

Putting the Schneider/Boston University New Product Launch Report findings to work starts with carving out a distinct launch phase in your new product development process. In this section, we'll cover the subprocesses within this new launch phase, along with the key step of assembling an integrated, dynamic launch team.

13

LAUNCH PHASE COMPONENTS

As we discussed back in Chapter 7, making launch a separate, distinct phase of your new product development process produces superior results. To show you how to do just that, in this chapter we'll introduce a modified version of Robert Cooper's widely used Stage-Gate® Process. For more than a decade and through several editions, *Winning at New Products: Accelerating the Process from Idea to Launch*, Cooper's treatise on the Stage-Gate Process, has served as the bible for new product developers in all kinds of industries.

According to the Product

"The reason a product is being launched should be seamless from product inception all the way through to when it gets into the consumers' hands. The best new products are developed from a consumer insight, but by the time they get launched, the message that goes to the consumer may no longer be based on the initial insight. Marketers sometimes go astray as they go along the Stage-Gate® Process. The product comes out differently from how it was originally conceived; it was designed for convenience and now it's being marketed for weight loss. Having the launch team involved early on in the process helps avoid this morphing of the message."

— *Fannie Young, Brand Manager for Schiefflin & Somerset, New York, New York*

Development & Management Association's best-practices study, 69 percent of the best new product developers in the United States employ some version of the multifunctional Stage-Gate Process;[1] this popularity is the reason we adopted the Stage-Gate Process as our working model. But we also know that some people doubt the efficacy of the Stage-Gate Process. We believe that making launch a separate phase significantly improves the outcome of the process. In addition, once you understand the subprocesses of the launch phase, you can easily adapt this phase to any new product development process.

The Stage-Gate Process divides the new product development effort into distinct, time-sequenced stages separated by management decision gates. The process includes five stages, with the last stage combining full production and market launch. Multifunctional teams must successfully complete a prescribed set of related cross-functional tasks in each stage before they obtain management approval to proceed to the next stage of product development. Here is Cooper's now-classic Stage-Gate Process:

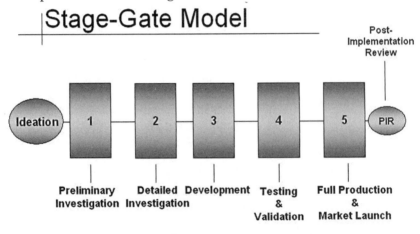

Cooper, R.G. and E. J. Kleinschmidt (1986), "An Investigation into the New Product Process: Steps, Deficiencies, and Impact," Journal of Product and Innovation Management, 3 (June), 71-85.

Modifying this model to allow for creation of a separate and highly focused launch stage involves changing Cooper's fifth stage from Full Production & Market Launch to just Full Production and adding a sixth stage labeled Market Launch. The dotted lines in the following revamped model indicate that some Market Launch activities must overlap other new product development stages and extend beyond the post implementation review. In other words, just because the launch stage falls at the end of the new product development process doesn't mean that all launch activities are on hold until the other stages are completed.

Launch Is A Separate Stage Gate

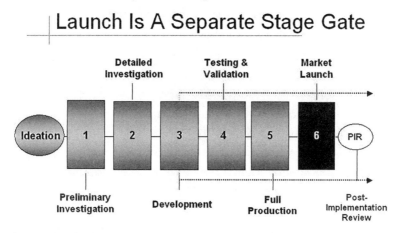

If you think about new product development as a huge jigsaw puzzle, one pivotal piece of the puzzle is launch. And that piece holds many important keys to figuring out the puzzle, which is why our new sixth stage of the Stage-Gate Process includes seven different components.

Schneider & Associates
Market Launch Stage Gate

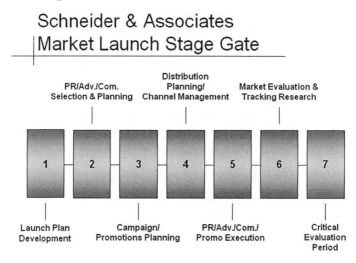

©2004 Schneider & Associates

The time frames in the following descriptions of each subprocess reflect data from companies that participated in the Schneider/Boston University New Product Launch Report. Because the majority of products were entirely new to the companies in the study, the time frames are not typical for line extension launches, which usually require less time.

PHASE 1 — LAUNCH PLAN DEVELOPMENT: While development of the overall launch plan usually begins as much as two years before final product shipment, finalization of the launch budget may not occur until 10 to 12 months before product shipment. In some cases, the budget changes over time in response to how well — or how badly — the launch is going. That's why launch plan development is the longest subcomponent of the Market Launch stage. The less successful products in the study tended to begin their launch planning far later than their business planning and budgeting, suggesting a strong focus on internal or financial matters at the expense of execution.

PHASE 2 — ADVERTISING/PR/COMMUNICATIONS AGENCY SELECTION AND PLANNING: Typically, companies bring in an ad agency quite early in the new product development process, often as far back as the original concept generation phase. This reflects the ongoing strategic relationships many ad agencies form with clients and their role in naming the product and developing its positioning. With public relations taking a lead role in more and more launches, though, it makes sense to also bring the PR agency on board as early as possible to help develop launch strategy.

PHASE 3 — CAMPAIGN/PROMOTIONS PLANNING: This is where the overall launch strategy is teased out into detailed, tactical plans for each component of the launch effort. For the more successful products in our study, such activities began 10 to 12 months before product rollout. For less successful products, however, PR planning didn't get under way until seven to nine months before ship date.

PHASE 4 — DISTRIBUTION PLANNING/CHANNEL MANAGEMENT: With these launch functions becoming more complex as the retail landscape continues to morph, earlier planning may be in order. In fact, the more successful products in our study were more likely to begin distribution planning and channel management activities approximately one year before final shipment, while their less successful counterparts waited until seven to nine months before shipment. We found that the latest trend is to take your "new product" to the retailer in its preliminary stage and ask the buyer to critique it. With this valuable input, you may find you have to reprice, repackage, or reformulate to meet retailer needs. But it's a lot less expensive to get this input before you've manufactured your product rather than after.

PHASE 5 — PR/ADVERTISING/COMMUNICATIONS/ PROMOTIONS EXECUTION: PR activity execution typically starts most launches, beginning within six months of shipment and lasting until as late as six months after the product rollout. Advertising and promotion activities tend to be executed in tandem, running from two to three months before shipment until four to six months after. Leading with PR, however, is far more effective in building early recognition and credibility than leading with advertising, as Al and Laura Ries show with case study after case study in *The Fall of Advertising & the Rise of PR*.

It's vital to carefully evaluate the optimum timeframe for executing the various launch plan components. Expert after expert told us that one of the most common — and biggest — mistakes they see is companies cutting their launch activities short by not starting them early enough and then by cutting them off too soon once the product is on store shelves. This approach doesn't provide enough time for launch messages to break through the clutter and reach target consumers. In addition, short campaigns allow no opportunity for tweaking strategies and messages if things don't go as well as hoped.

PHASE 6 — MARKET EVALUATION AND TRACKING RESEARCH: This phase covers the period of close evaluation before you make major decisions about the product's future. Evaluation research takes place four to six months before shipment and often lasts until one to two years after a launch campaign. Before shipment, companies are looking at their channel distribution to determine if they have enough product to satisfy demand, or perhaps too much product based on the number of orders. After the product is shipped, companies closely watch sales to weigh whether they should produce more product, or slow or stop production based on limited sales. If companies have line extensions planned for a product line, this is when they consider whether to begin production on the new-and-improved version or on additional models, flavors, or styles, or whether to wait and see if the original product takes off.

PHASE 7 — CRITICAL EVALUATION PERIOD: In the Schneider/Boston University New Product Launch Report, the average period devoted to judging product viability was six months. That's surprisingly short, considering the purchase cycles of many products. The time needed to break through the marketing clutter and achieve the all-important sustainability discussed in Chapter 1 far exceeds six months for many types of products. And any launch that doesn't take into consideration the amount of time needed to build a loyal customer base in its product category is bound to fail.

In our study, the critical evaluation phase tended to start earlier and last longer for the less successful products (from shipment date until 10 to 12 months after) than for the more successful products (two to three months after shipment until seven to nine months after). This longer period was likely a function of the organizations' attempts to determine reasons for lower-than-expected success. Companies are often loath to admit failure, so they may wait to take a product off the shelf until they either have another to replace it or until retailers pull the plug.

In our current research, we've heard that retailers are yanking products off the shelves in 90 days if they don't perform to standards. This quest for instantly successful products is unrealistic and unfair. Yes, shelf space is precious, but consumer demand takes time to build. Retailers need to help manufacturers call attention to their new products, because it's in everyone's best interest to find a way to help new products succeed.

In Chapter 28, we'll introduce an invaluable tool for analyzing what has gone astray with a launch, a practice called After Action Reviews. Adapted from the military, this methodology can help you craft on-the-fly improvements to launch that should boost results. It can also provide reconnaissance that will make future launches more successful from the get-go.

Stage-Gate® in Motion

The Schwan Food Company, headquartered in Marshall, Minnesota, is the largest branded frozen-food company in the United States, with 24,000 employees. In addition to its Schwan's Home Service, which is the nation's largest direct-to-home food service, the company produces frozen foods under such well-known brand names as Tony's®, Red Baron®, Freschetta®, Edwards®, and Mrs. Smith's®.

In 2003, Schwan implemented the Stage-Gate® Process to guide its new product development efforts. Coordinating the implementation was new product process director Steve Linstrom, an eight-year Schwan veteran. And while the companywide effort was still maturing, Linstrom was enthusiastic about the process's potential.

"The Stage-Gate Process spotlights improvement opportunities," he said. "For example, we didn't have our product strategy as well defined and integrated as it could be, so when the Stage-Gate Process required us to make a strategic fit at each gate, we bounced around a little. We're driving towards doing a better job of identifying our strategies exactly. That will allow us to do portfolio management, and Stage-Gate will help us monitor how well we're doing that. It enables us to tie projects to our strategy."

About 320 Schwan employees have learned to use the Stage-Gate Process. A two-day training session featured a half-day lecture and then an interactive activity in which cross-functional teams wrote integrated product definitions, presented them to the entire class, and then devised project plans and business cases for the group to evaluate. Additional quarterly training sessions will introduce new employees to the process.

"From a tactical side, it has worked well for us; it has forced better communications between the various entities working on projects," said Linstrom. "It's more of a communication tool than anything else, helping you make sure you're not missing anything. It also brings accountability to the process. We were already doing many of the things in the process, but now we're writing them down and sharing them with everybody else; that creates greater accountability."

The process forces Schwan's cross-functional teams to develop a finalized, integrated product definition early in Stage-Gate 2. Using the Cooper method, the team defines the target market and states why they need the product and why they don't need the product.

"In our training sessions," said Linstrom, "that is where the light comes on because R&D is thinking a product definition is the specifications, marketing thinks about how the product is different, and manufacturing is thinking about how we are going to make it.

"By creating the integrated definition, freezing it, and having it hang over the heads of everybody through the process, you're committing to it and not making it up as you go along. As a result, the market launch plan talks about the product's specific goals and ties them all the way back to that integrated product definition. We were doing this in the past, but not everyone got to see what the plan was."

Schwan's process includes creating a preliminary launch plan at Stage-Gate 3. A representative of the sales group also participates at Stage-Gates 3, 4, and 5 to add a sales perspective to the process.

"We found that the launch has been kind of an afterthought for us, so we're trying to correct that by starting to plan that in Stage-Gate 3," said Linstrom.

Linstrom believes using Stage-Gate is helping the company eliminate process "silos."

"That's one of its biggest benefits," he said. "It helps everyone look at the product strategically. Instead of just thinking, 'I have to get this egg roll out of here,' you're thinking, 'This is for this customer segment and this is why they need this.' You improve your chances of having a successful product."

14

DEVELOPING A LAUNCH BRIEF

Launch Strategy #3 stresses the importance of having a launch plan. A good first step toward developing that plan is preparing a document called a Launch Brief, which will guide internal and external launch team members through the planning process. This is a short summary — only two to three pages — that helps launch partners understand the task at hand. All of the creative agencies can then build their launch strategy based on the criteria you develop. At Schneider & Associates, we use the Launch Brief as the basis for Idea Camp™, a brainstorming process we've developed to generate highly creative starter ideas for launch planning. You'll learn all about Idea Camp in Section 6.

We realize that many companies are fond of giving the launch team three-ring binders bulging with information at the start of a project. But how many launch team members really read all that data? With a two- to three-page document, though, everyone can zip through because it's simple, it's clear, and they can read it over and over to be sure their strategy is on target. Boiling things down to the essential task at hand is a much more effective way to get everyone on the same page.

There are lots of variations on what you can put in your Launch Brief. The information categories may differ slightly from product to product, but the basics should include:

- **TARGET:** Who do we want to talk to?

- **PURPOSE:** What do we want them to do? (This is a deceptively simple question, and the correct answer is *not* "Buy our new product." Depending on the nature of your product, you may be asking people to change a habit, jump aboard a trend, or accept a whole new technology. So define exactly what you are asking consumers to do.)

- **CURRENT RESPONSE:** What are consumers saying about our brand now, before we start advertising and publicizing this new product? If a competitor has a similar product on the market, what are people saying about that product? (The Internet can be an invaluable listening post for gathering the information you need to answer this question.)

- **DESIRED RESPONSE:** What do we want consumers to say about our brand and about this product as a result of the launch campaign? How will this product enhance our brand?

- **BENEFITS:** What does this new product offer our target market? What problem are we helping consumers solve? What goals are we helping them achieve? How are we making their lives easier/better?

- **SUPPORT:** What will we do to support the launch? How will this launch support the brand?

- **PERSONALITY:** What is the personality of the brand? What kind of car would it drive? What kind of clothes would it wear? What kind of music would it listen to? What kind of friends would it have? Ask lifestyle questions about the personality of the brand as a way to determine what the launch campaign should look and feel like.

- **MARKET TRENDS:** What is happening in the target market that impacts this launch, both positively and negatively?

- **COMPETITIVE FRAMEWORK:** Who are we competing against? What are they doing to market their products?

- **EXECUTION CONSIDERATIONS:** What are the chief hurdles for this launch? Are there any significant limitations that need to be considered during planning?

Obviously, this is a lot of information to squeeze into three pages, so the answers to these questions need to be succinct. A bulleted list works best. What you want in the end is a document communicating the essence of the launch task that can be easily digested, thoroughly understood, and agreed upon by everyone.

Benefits of the Launch Brief

Here's what the Launch Brief accomplishes:

- It clarifies internal thinking about the launch. First and foremost, preparing the Launch Brief helps the internal launch team come together around what they truly want to accomplish with the launch. Any underlying misconceptions or differences of opinion are exposed, and a consensus can be established. This is a big step toward avoiding problems when external team members are brought into the process. If there's a conflict among internal team members, the external team members will almost always hear different messages. Then, the external team members will be slowed by false starts and misdirection as they try to figure out who is really in charge and whose opinion to heed. The Launch Brief can eliminate all this confusion.

- It can expose weaknesses in the new product. Preparing a Launch Brief should not be all that difficult for a truly good new product. If you're having a hard time answering basic questions about the product benefits and how the product will enhance your brand, alarm bells should go off. It may be time to go back to the drawing board and evaluate whether launching this product at this time is a smart move. We have all seen cases where companies launched products that were so far afield from their existing brand image that it made us ask, "What were they thinking?" We've also witnessed plenty of new products that had no real differentiating message or benefit. Given the high failure rates of new products, it is clearly possible for an ill-conceived new product to make it to market without anyone in-house blowing the whistle and saying, "Hey, this is a dumb idea!" The Launch Brief is an opportunity for people to put their heads together and come to just that conclusion — even if it hurts to do so.

• It assures that everyone is working from the same page. The Launch Brief starts everyone out with the same basic information and acts as the launch communications touchstone. As the launch team digs deeper into the planning process, they will no doubt want more in-depth information about various aspects of the Launch Brief — that's where the bulging three-ring binder comes in handy. But by giving them a concise grounding tool at the start, you're assured that all of the launch partners are working within the same framework.

• It helps establish true team integration. Let's face it: Competition runs rampant among the various agencies brought on board for a launch. It's hard to avoid territorialism because everyone naturally wants the biggest slice of the project pie. But sometimes that competition is unwittingly fostered by companies that treat agencies differently when it comes to access to information and internal team members.

If you begin the launch planning process by bringing everyone together to present the Launch Brief, the agencies know they are starting off on a level playing field in terms of the information available to them. In addition, they all benefit by participating in an open and honest discussion generated by the Launch Brief. This process goes a long way toward getting the team off to the right start so it functions as a single unit, rather than individual — and often competing — units working to benefit their own self interests rather than the good of the launch.

• It serves as an evaluation tool as planning proceeds. All plans coming from the various creative agencies should be evaluated in the context of the Launch Brief. Does the ad campaign have the look and feel of what we set forth for this launch? Does the PR campaign focus on the product benefits that we outlined in the Launch Brief? Is the product spokesperson we're considering really a good fit with our target consumer and the brand's personality? Does the Web site offer our target audience something unique?

By constantly using the Launch Brief as a measuring stick during the entire launch planning process, you can guard against your message morphing into something else. Message morphing happens when the reasons (i.e., consumer benefits) a product was developed get lost or muddled as the product is handed off from the development team to the launch team. That's why it's important to have people from the development team participate in creating the Launch Brief.

Next, we turn to one of the most important steps in the launch process — selecting the external members of your launch team. We'll also tell you more about how to create solid working relationships with the agencies that are going to help you achieve the objectives you've outlined in your Launch Brief.

15

CHOOSING YOUR LAUNCH PARTNERS

Deciding on your traveling companions for your challenging journey to launch success is a critical part of the Market Launch Stage-Gate. Making wise choices at this stage will help you take advantage of the power of our next Launch Strategy.

Launch Strategy #6:
Assemble an Expert Launch Crew

"If you're doing a joint promotion with another company, make sure you allow enough time to foster a relationship with your partner. Even within straight launch promotions, having enough time to develop the program, sell it in through your own sales force, and then gain shelf space is critical."

— *Chris Donnelly, President of GeigerDonnelly Marketing LLC, Foxboro, Massachusetts*

You may already have ongoing relationships with some of the creative firms that will make up the external components of your launch team. But it's always a good idea to review these relationships in light of the Launch Brief to ensure that your current partners have the experience and skills needed to fulfill the launch task you've set forth.

If you feel you need some fresh thinking on the team, or if you don't already have existing agency relationships, you'll want to go through a search process. Creating your Launch Brief is actually a good first step for this process. The information you assemble for the Launch Brief prepares you to answer the questions any smart agency will ask before they develop a proposal for you. In fact, if they're not asking the kinds of questions you answered in the Launch Brief, they don't have what it takes to make your launch a success.

As Jim Collins says in his book *Good to Great,* "It's not just about assembling the right team — that's nothing new. The main point is to first get the right people on the bus (and the wrong people off the bus) before you figure out where to drive it."[1]

Agency Essentials

Before you start your agency search, decide what qualifications and qualities you're seeking in external launch partners. Here's a short list of the basic characteristics an agency needs to serve you effectively; depending on the nature of your launch, you may want to expand this list to include other traits.

• **LAUNCH KNOWLEDGE:** Most agencies have experience in launching new products or services, but you'll want to carefully evaluate the depth of this experience. For instance, doing a national rollout is significantly more complex than doing a regional launch, so if yours is a national launch, you'll probably want advertising and PR firms that have worked at this level. Don't be afraid to consider agencies that have done launches in industries other than yours. Sometimes the crossover knowledge they bring to the table is helpful in spurring ideas for a new approach that hasn't been tried in your field. The result could be a launch with a totally fresh look and feel.

• **SUPERIOR CREATIVITY:** Nowhere is a high degree of creativity more essential than when conducting a new product launch. And the bigger your launch challenge, the more creativity you want your external partners to exhibit. Breaking through the media and retail clutter to grab consumers' attention requires innovative, even bold ideas. Look for partners whose concepts surprise and delight you.

- **TIMELINESS & AGILITY:** The ability to meet deadlines is all-important in a launch program. All program elements have to flow seamlessly; you can't afford to have a weak link agency on your team that doesn't work in a timely fashion. Likewise, following the success strategy of not setting your launch plan in stone means you want your agency partners to be agile enough to easily adapt to schedule and market changes.

> **"If you look at the power** of third-party endorsements and the fragmentation of communication channels, the most powerful method of communication today is the power of word of mouth. The way 'conversation' is generated is through thoughtful understanding of the product or service, and this is what PR people are the best trained to do. They understand the incredible attributes of a product or service and know how to make it engaging or exciting to core stakeholders. PR people need to be at the table from the start so they can help craft what's going to be said about the product and get people talking about it."
>
> — *Carol Cone, Chief Executive Officer of Cone, Inc., Boston, Massachusetts*

- **BUDGET CONSCIOUSNESS:** Your agency partners should treat your money as if it were their own. When you're checking a prospective agency's references, a question about how the agency handles budgets should be high on your list.

- **CONFIDENTIALITY:** Hearing bad news about the agency's other clients from agency personnel should set off a red alert in your mind. A good agency shouldn't make you wonder if information about your business is being shared with others.

A Different Mindset, A Different Philosophy

Choosing the internal members of your launch team is, of course, every bit as important as selecting the best external partners possible. The Schneider/Boston University New Product Launch Report included one question that provides interesting insight into the internal selection process: We asked people to choose descriptors that best characterized the product launch process. The responses, shown in the following table, suggest that launch is a unique business/marketing process, one that requires a particular attitude and philosophy and, accordingly, a different set of skills among managers.

LAUNCH CHARACTERISTICS*

	Total %	Highly Successful Launches	Less Successful Launches
Exciting	50%	63%	38%
Creative	46	57	35
Rewarding	46	57	35
Proactive	43	53	32
Systematic	22	29	14
Evolutionary	19	29	5
Synergistic	20	26	14
Ego-involving	24	20	32
Reactive	22	18	30
Political	21	14	32
Unpredictable	14	10	22

*Top responses to the question asking respondents to choose from descriptors that best characterize the product launch process.

The differences between highly successful product launches and less successful launches are worth noting. Highly successful product launches were much more apt to be described as exciting, creative, rewarding, and proactive experiences than were their less successful counterparts. The launch activities of highly successful products were also more apt to be characterized as evolutionary, systematic, and synergistic, while those of less successful products were more likely to be described as reactive, unpredictable, political, and ego-involving.

There's no way to know how much the responses to this question were influenced by the success or failure of the launch in which survey participants had participated. And it's not terribly surprising that people involved in less successful launches were more negative in their choices of descriptors. What can be said about this list is that it provides excellent clues you can use when recruiting the ideal personality profile for an internal launch team member. In other words, you're looking for people who can get excited about the product and its launch, who are creative, proactive, and systematic about their work. You're also seeking people who think out of the box and are therefore capable of developing an evolutionary campaign that stretches the boundaries of what the company has done before.

Avoid recruiting people who take a reactive versus a proactive approach to assignments, or who are overly fond of office politics. Also steer clear of ego-driven managers who can't work synergistically with others because they are so self-absorbed in promoting their own ideas.

Here's a final bit of good advice from management guru Jim Collins: "What do the right people want more than anything else? They want to be part of a winning team. They want to contribute to producing visible, tangible results. They want to feel the excitement of being involved in something that just flat-out works. When the right people see a simple plan born of confronting the brutal facts — a plan developed from understanding, not bravado — they are likely to say, 'That'll work, count me in.'"[2]

Conducting an Agency Search

A well-designed agency search achieves two purposes. It helps you:

- find a firm that can provide superior ideas, execution, and results.

- start the formation of a strong client/agency relationship.

This means that in addition to evaluating the professional capabilities of potential agencies, you also want to get to know your prospective partners and give them a chance to get to know you. You want to come away from the process with a sense of what it would be like to work together, often for many hours of the day. Building into your search the face-to-face interaction required for learning about each other can lengthen the process, but it's well worth it in the end. Nothing is worse than choosing an agency and then finding out that the firm's personality just isn't a match for your organization's culture. A launch can be a long voyage; make sure you're traveling with people who know how to navigate the terrain and who will be fun to spend time with on the journey.

Let's look at some basic steps for conducting an agency search that will help you achieve the two aims listed earlier:

• Using your Launch Brief as a guide to articulate your needs, create a list of potential agency candidates. You can draw these from a number of sources. The Internet can be exceedingly useful for helping you reach beyond those firms you already know. Look at case studies on the Web sites for firms that have done campaigns you've admired. An agency Web site's ability to clearly, creatively communicate a mission speaks volumes about whether that agency should be on your list or not. Call companies whose launches you've followed and ask about their agencies. Talk to people at the local ad club or a nearby chapter of the Public Relations Society of America (www.prsa.org). Check on-line directories of ad and PR firms that might yield the perfect agency for your launch. Trade editors, too, are often good sources of information on which companies and agencies do an excellent job of launching new products.

The Council of Public Relations Firms, a professional group made up of more than 100 leading PR agencies in the United States, recommends keeping this initial search list to no more than eight firms.

• For the initial screening process, provide the prospective agencies with basic information on your launch project, including a ballpark budget and the scope of the work. Ask them to respond with information on their firm and its relevant experience. At this stage, do not overburden agencies with requests for unnecessary information; you want them to be able to prepare a response in a fairly short period of time. What you mainly want to do is gauge their interest in your project and learn a little about who they are and if they are qualified to handle your launch. Obtaining client and former client references is also advisable at this stage.

• Review the submissions from the agencies on your long list and contact their references. Ask the references to evaluate the agencies based on the criteria mentioned earlier in this chapter. If you're speaking to a former client of the agency, ask why they no longer work together and whether they would select the agency again if the need arose. Ask if the agency team worked well together and with the client's team. Ask if they're fun to work with!

Judge the materials submitted by the agencies based on creativity and on how clearly they communicate. Consider what kind of agency personality is beginning to peek through in the way the materials speak to you. Pay special attention to each firm's marketing brochure. The creativity and clarity of message an agency brings to its own marketing materials — the one time it is totally free of client constraints — can be a strong indicator of the quality of its work for you.

With the advent of the Internet, agencies also use Web sites to showcase their work and convey their personality. In some cases, the Web site has replaced expensive printed marketing brochures, so if an agency on your list doesn't have a brochure, make sure you look at the Web site to see if the firm's individuality resonates with the personality of your brand and organization.

• Narrow the list to three or four agencies and go visit them. As Walter Mills, principal and chief operating officer of PART-NERS+simons, a Boston communications firm, advises, "An agency's lair is very revealing. It will tell you a lot about how they do business, how they treat people, and, if you look carefully, how much the people there enjoy their jobs." Mills also advises asking about workplace churn, since you want to be sure a large portion of the staff has significant tenure. With a launch that's going to stretch out over a year or more, you don't want to have to keep breaking in new agency team members every few months.

While you're at the agency, ask to meet the professionals you'll work with day-to-day on the launch. Often these individuals aren't on the agency's new business team, but they are the people who will be integral to accomplishing the agency's work on your behalf. So make sure you're meeting not only the people who are skilled at selling business, but also the ones who are going to do the business of developing the creative work.

• Provide the agencies on the short list with an opportunity to demonstrate their strategic thinking about your launch. This is where things sometimes get sticky. You want to make the creative assignment significant enough to allow you to intelligently evaluate the agencies, but you don't want to overburden them with time-consuming work or use this phase as a way to simply get free ideas for your launch.

To avoid problems, make sure your creative assignment is limited and well focused. At this point, we recommend narrowing the field to two candidates. That way, the agencies know they have a solid chance of getting your business and will be more willing to make the necessary investment in time and creative work. Also, consider compensating these final candidates for their creative concepts and ideas. This is a huge agency motivator and shows your commitment to the process.

• Meet with the finalists again. Discuss your response to how they completed the creative assignment. Ask for their thoughts on your launch challenge; a top-notch agency will have done a lot of homework by now and should be able to offer solid insights into your situation. This is a good chance to get more of a feel for what it would be like to work together.

• Make your choice. Call the agency you're selecting with the good news. Don't forget to let the other candidates down nicely. Give them productive feedback on why they weren't selected. Every agency wants to understand why you chose a competitor, so any information you can offer makes them more effective at the next pitch. In addition, you never know when another launch assignment will come along that another candidate would be perfect for, so you want to leave these relationships in good standing. Nothing makes an agency's new business team crazier than a prospective client who leaves them hanging and doesn't report the search results in a polite, timely fashion.

In the next chapter, we'll look at getting your relationship with your launch partners off on the right track. Aligning everyone from the start can play a major role in your launch success.

16

ALIGNING THE LAUNCH TEAM

The way you start off your relationship with your creative firms can be critical in determining whether you and your external partners live happily ever after. The first step toward success is getting everyone aboard the launch ship and rowing in the same direction. This is the time to host a team alignment meeting or a new account startup session.

Thoroughly discuss the Launch Brief with the creative firms. While you may have shared this document in the agency search process, you'll want to delve into it more deeply at the team alignment meeting. It's important to share all the data about your company, its competitors, your concerns about the launch — get it all out on the table so the launch team can be prepared for any eventuality. It's always better to anticipate problems than to discover a lot of "surprises" during the launch process.

Create an open atmosphere to encourage an exchange of ideas. Make sure your outside partners feel free to question Launch Brief assumptions that they may have hesitated to ask about during the search process.

You may want to revise the Launch Brief based on your external partners' input. They may bring to the table information about competitors that you didn't have, for example. Or they may have knowledge about another industry that is directly transferable to your launch. Make sure you take advantage of all of the expertise you've gathered around the table to produce a final Launch Brief that represents the best thinking available.

This is also an organizational session at which you'll establish:

- **A COMPLETE "DATA DUMP."** Now is the time to haul out that heavy three-ring binder with all the information you've been accumulating about your product, its competition, and the marketplace. Take time to highlight the data you found exciting in terms of formulating a launch strategy. Encourage the agencies to review the material and then come back with their own insights. Part of the benefit of working with external partners is having fresh eyes look at information you've been living with throughout the product development process.

- **DIVISION OF RESPONSIBILITIES.** Discuss who will do what, since there is usually some overlap in capabilities among the agencies on a launch team. The agencies should respect and defer to each other's core competencies. Things can get dicey if this doesn't happen, but as Walter Mills of PARTNERS+simons told us, "While collaborators are often cross-functional to some extent, each must give up the right to challenge the expertise of the others to help engineer successful problem solving as a collaborative group. Professional, disciplined discussions and free exchanges are at the heart of all successful collaborations."

- **PRELIMINARY PROJECT TIMETABLES.** Establish the initial timeline for completing the other phases of the Market Launch Stage-Gate. Make sure the agencies know about the launch success factors that involve keeping plans flexible and learning to live with inevitable delays. Discuss the implications of these success factors with regard to your own launch. Alert the agencies about where along the launch path you anticipate delays. Promise to keep them abreast of developments that impact their work and the timetable.

- **LAUNCH OBJECTIVES.** If you haven't already done so, decide now what success will look like for your new product and share that with everyone on the launch team. What are the metrics you'll use to measure success? How long will the product be in distribution before you declare success or failure? The answers to such questions will vary depending on the nature of your new product, but whatever your criteria, it is essential to set them in advance.

Having this measuring stick helps your external agencies understand the kinds of results you expect their programs to achieve. Equally important, it greatly streamlines your internal decision-making process as the launch moves forward. With no success criteria in hand, it's all too easy to rationalize throwing good money after bad if a launch isn't going as well as you had hoped; establishing success metrics in advance helps eliminate this tendency.

• **THE APPROVAL PROCESS.** What is the system for getting creative materials approved? Who has the ultimate sign-off? The more orderly you can make the approvals process, the better. Just as too many cooks produce a bland soup, too many editors can take all the individuality and punch out of your copy, and too many creative directors can devastate your launch visuals. Make sure you speak to your external launch partners with one voice, not many.

• **CONTACT PEOPLE IN EACH ORGANIZATION.** Resolve questions about how your organization and the various agencies will interact. By dealing with these issues up front, you will avoid confusion and misunderstandings once you get your launch program on track. It's best to create a sheet with everyone's pertinent information, including home phones, cell phones, and work and personal e-mail addresses. You never know when you will have to call someone to meet an emergency deadline, so this directory sheet is imperative.

• **PREFERRED COMMUNICATION METHODS.** Let your agencies know what your preferences are for receiving communications. Do you like phone calls or e-mail? Do you expect daily or weekly written updates on progress, and should those come via e-mail or fax?

- **BILLING ISSUES.** If your company has specific requirements on how invoicing is to be done, let your agencies know this up front. This is also the time to decide on the procedure for signing off on necessary budget changes; in addition, establish a limit on direct expense spending that an agency can undertake on your behalf without receiving prior approval from you.

Eliminate the Silos!

We had been working for a consumer products company for four years, launching new products and handling crisis communications and trade relations. One day, our client invited us to a meeting to discuss the launch of a very important new product line, one that would revolutionize their brand and business. Attending the meeting was a branding firm that, unbeknownst to us, had been working with our client for six years!

At the meeting, the internal and external marketing group struggled to get its arms around the launch messaging and timing for the product. It was a tough task because the product's formula was in constant flux, and the result of a formula change could greatly impact the product positioning and messaging. After going in circles for several hours, we suggested the branding partner and our firm meet off-line to develop suggestions to bring back to the client marketing group at a later date.

When we gathered with the branding firm to brainstorm, we couldn't believe we had never met before. When we asked what they had been doing for the client, they told us they had created all the product messaging, sell sheets, and packaging — all tools that we used to write our press materials.

This was not the first time we'd been surprised to learn long after the fact that a client had other marketing resources that we had not been told about. How does this happen? Are marketing managers' minds so compartmentalized that they don't think one agency needs to talk to another? Do they think it is going to cost more if we confer? We think it would cost less!

In this case, the branding and PR team, with the help of a facilitator, created the entire schematic for the launch and many of the key messages in just four hours. In our experience, the synergies created by having people from the different marketing disciplines work together far exceed the cost and the time involved when the creatives work apart from each other. Get rid of those silos that keep launch team agencies from communicating and reap the benefits of a truly integrated marketing team that is able to create a truly integrated launch.

As an aside, when we asked the client why she had not brought her creative partners together regularly, she said, "First and foremost, the launches you've been involved in so far were line extensions, requiring little communication strategy and roll-out planning because they were strategically aligned with the existing brand and could play off the existing toolbox.

"In the case of the new product (or any other true new product launch), clearly it's more powerful to connect the best and the brightest early in the process," she added. "This allows collective thinking, but more importantly, fuels the entire process by sharing the energy and knowledge base of all disciplines. The up-front time and energy pays off in the end when all teams are in alignment and have shared in the process."

Keep in Close Touch

Regularly scheduled launch team meetings are essential to building a strong, productive client-agency relationship. In addition to giving you a chance to review and revise your launch content and timetable, these sessions also allow you to update your external partners on developments — both good and bad — that may affect the launch plan. Use e-mail and the telephone to communicate on an ad hoc basis as new opportunities or problems arise, but understand the value of face-to-face meetings for gaining insight and consensus and for keeping the launch team aligned. At the very least, we suggest weekly scheduled phone conferences so everyone stays on the same page.

It's also important to be totally candid with your external partners when you are dissatisfied with some aspect of their work. Make sure the lines of communication are always open when it comes to what you expect from them and — equally important — what they expect from you. Make sure you tell them specifically what you don't like so they can correct the creative, the staffing, or the account service.

Make a habit of questioning your agency contacts about issues that affect their ability to do a good job, such as whether they have all the information they need to write your launch materials, or if your internal approval process is working smoothly and in a timely fashion.

As with any relationship involving money, budgets can become a major source of misunderstandings. To avoid these problems, establish a clear understanding of budget constraints at the start of any work, and be certain agency personnel know you want to hear about budget overruns *before* they occur, not after.

PREPARING FOR IGNITION

Now that your team is assembled, it's time to develop the individual elements of a launch campaign that will successfully meet the objectives you've set. With thousands of new products screaming for attention, your launch team needs to maximize the creativity and effectiveness of your strategy and launch plan components. This section will discuss how you can accomplish this important mission.

17

How It's Usually Done

n the public relations world, the traditional paradigm for developing a new product launch plan goes something like this:

1. A company invites its PR agency (or a prospective PR agency) to a meeting. The client tells the group it has set a launch date for an exciting new product, usually within three to six months. The agency is hearing about this new product for the first time, and the PR professionals are given two or three hours to learn about the product and the company's goals and to ask questions. Keep in mind that this product may have been in devel-

> **"You can learn from** other people's mistakes and even your own. People don't pay enough attention to what's happened before; there is a wealth of knowledge in this business, no different from the stock market. Some products are extremely successful, and some need to be revamped, and some were launched improperly. Learn from those successes and those mistakes."
>
> — *John Rattigan, Director of Marketing and Business Development for Colorado Boxed Beef Company, Auburndale, Florida*

opment for as long as two years, and the company has spent millions of dollars on its production. There are probably rooms full of information about the product, why it was developed, and other pertinent data. But the company will share very little of this treasure trove with its agency or potential agency.

2. The PR team returns to its office, reads the information it has been given, and develops a plan, a time line, and a budget based on the client meeting. In addition, the firm usually conducts third-party research or calls to beg the ad agency or market research firm for the studies they've conducted on the client's behalf.

3. The PR agency enthusiastically presents its plan to the client, who decides the plan is "off strategy" and wonders why.

4. The company either decides to help the agency see the light or keeps interviewing agencies until one of them appears with a plan that seems to have been created with a crystal ball — or perhaps divine intervention.

5. Whichever firm the company selects, critical time is wasted tinkering with the plan before actual implementation — precious time that could be spent executing the plan, not just thinking about it.

This strategy for launch briefings and agency selection is also widely used with promotional firms, Web site developers, and other key players on the launch team, so everything we're about to say applies to them as well.

Why This Model Doesn't Work

This well-established path to launch plan creation has several tragic flaws. We'll look at three key problems: timing, the need for information, and the importance of having a truly integrated launch team.

1. It's Too Darn Late

Not educating external partners about a new product until you've already set a launch date is a recipe for failure. In our experience, word that the client is launching a new product or service often arrives at our door excruciatingly close to the actual launch date. Companies that overlook the key success strategy of treating launch as a separate phase are more prone to this self-defeating behavior.

Here's one example of how close some companies get to the launch date before calling in the launch troops. When Pepperidge Farm Inc. approached Schneider & Associates about relaunching Smiley the Goldfish®, we were thrilled at the opportunity. One of America's icon products, this adorable snack cracker was celebrating its 35th anniversary. The Pepperidge Farm engineers had even figured out how to put a smile on the Goldfish to delight both moms and school-age kids, their key target audiences, and the happy cracker was scheduled to launch during back-to-school season. What fun!

There was, however, one catch: 350,000 cases of grinning Goldfish were already in the warehouse, ready to be shipped. To meet the deadlines for what was planned as a back-to-school launch, we had two weeks to develop the program and six weeks to execute it. Since Pepperidge Farm's R&D had worked on technology to put a smile on the Goldfish for 10 years, you'd think they would have begun launch planning just a tad earlier.

Okay, so some companies cut things a little close, and launch teams have to kick into overdrive, working long hours to create and execute a launch strategy. Is that such a disaster?

It sure is. The Schneider/Boston University New Product Launch Report showed that highly successful products began the public relations process 10 to 12 months before the ship date. In contrast, less successful products started planning their public relations efforts just seven to nine months prior to the ship date. Unfortunately, the Pepperidge Farm situation is not an aberration. We've seen case after case in which companies tried to compress the launch process to ridiculously short periods — even down to two months before launch. These tightened timetables lead to less than optimum results at best, and to disasters at worst.

Allowing adequate time for launch planning and execution is especially critical if you've got a breakthrough product. Breakthrough products need breakthrough public relations launch strategies, Web sites, and other promotional campaigns. Developing anything out of the ordinary takes more time, both to create the ideas and to effectively execute them.

Breaking Through Competitive Clutter Takes Time

With ever-growing numbers of new products seeking media attention, a great deal is riding on your ability to break through the competitive clutter. Getting on the radar screens of the print and broadcast media is critical. Internet story placements may operate at warp speed, but it still takes time to pitch and schedule the other major media placements that consumer companies want.

To secure placements in major monthly magazines, for example, you need to start pitching editors at least five to six months before the newsstand date. For a major morning show trend or feature segment, you must demonstrate to the producer or reporter as much as two to three months in advance that you have a piece that fits into his or her format (and you often have to promise an exclusive). Of course, placing print and broadcast news coverage takes less time, but if you are going to persuade a reporter to write a major news feature, count on two weeks at least. Newspapers, magazines, and television stations want to promote a big story, so they need time to work their own marketing magic.

As Al Ries and Laura Ries point out in *The Fall of Advertising & the Rise of PR*, "PR programs are inevitably linear. One thing leads to another. In a linear program, the elements unfold over time … in fact, if you're launching a new brand with a PR program, you have no choice. You have to use a slow buildup, as there is no way you can coordinate media coverage. You start small, often with a mention of the brand in some obscure publication. Then you roll out the program to more important media."[1] These linear, slow-building programs take time, but time is exactly what many companies don't give their external partners.

As we mentioned earlier, the Rieses make a strong case in their book that PR, rather than advertising, should drive brand-building strategy. If this is true, and we certainly believe it is, then calling in the PR pros near the very end of the product development process makes no sense. A better plan would be to give the entire launch team an opportunity to contribute ideas about the product at a time when their input can still make a difference.

Now, asking the whole launch team for input would no doubt be a controversial notion at some companies. Many new product development professionals would say they don't need help from external marketing folks, thank you very much. But the obvious question, then, is why do the vast majority of new products fail? Listening to the viewpoints of the key players deputized to deliver your new product message to the media surely can't hurt, can it?

Sooner IS Better

Many of the marketing executives we interviewed who had launched highly successful products said they brought their advertising and other agencies on board early in the process. Sometimes the agencies joined the internal team as far back as three or more years before the product's shipping date. This agency/client integration is indicative of the ongoing strategic relationships many ad agencies and some PR firms have with their clients.

Clearly, the ad agency or graphic design firm needs to be on board first so they can develop the brand image for the product. The brand platform, the logo, the tag line, the packaging — all need to be created early in the process. But here's where we think having the entire team strategize together adds value.

To give an example, let's go back to the Pepperidge Farm smiling Goldfish project. The packaging, designed months before the ad agency was hired or we were brought on board to develop the public relations campaign, included a $25,000 photo contest on the back. No one had considered how this contest might be leveraged in the advertising or public relations campaigns, and because we were added to the team so late, we didn't have enough time to organize a photography tie-in that made sense. In this case, the contest ended up being a stand-alone promotion that wasn't reinforced by advertising or PR — a wasted opportunity, as far as we're concerned.

Our question is, what takes companies so long to bring the PR and promotional teams on board to craft the launch strategy? Are brand and marketing managers phobic about paying too many consultants simultaneously? Are they afraid the consultants are going to disagree and then production will be held up?

2. Too Little Information Is Provided

Another flaw in the old launch paradigm is that it's impossible to learn everything you need to know to develop an effective, results-oriented launch plan in just one or two meetings. This is especially true when the product being launched is truly unique and not just a line extension. No matter how familiar an agency is with the client's product mix and its market, if there's something ground-breaking in the works, a short meeting will only skim the surface of the product or service, the nuances of the category, and the market.

What also happens frequently is that the PR representatives are handed an armful of market research and other in-depth information as they leave the room after the briefing. The product managers, who could provide the most valuable information, are so busy getting the product out the door that they resist taking time to answer questions as the agency team tries to decipher the information before moving into brainstorming mode.

In contrast, ad agency representatives sit behind two-way mirrors with clients, listening to multiple consumer focus groups, and attend meetings where the market research firm interprets the focus group results. The PR firm then gets the briefing books without the firsthand knowledge of what the research firm revealed to the client. Our advice: Invite key consultants to the focus groups. The information they learn firsthand from consumers is critical to creating a launch campaign that resonates with the people who are going to buy your product.

Too often, the internal team members who are most knowledgeable about the new product, its launch objectives, the challenges, and the market are not in the room when the creative thinking about the launch campaign takes place. Inside the room, instead, are public relations professionals who've known about the product for only a week, wracking their brains to create a launch plan that will capture the attention of consumers.

3. The Team Isn't Really a Team

This leads us to another significant problem: Creating a launch plan often isn't an integrated team effort, because two or more teams are working separately — the client, the ad agency, the PR firm, and others. Too often, the team organizational meeting we described in Chapter 16 never happens. Again, the PR agency develops a creative plan in a vacuum, without any real client participation in the actual creative part of the process. Then when the creative strategies are presented, it's not surprising that the client sometimes thinks the ideas are off base.

18

DOING IT A BETTER WAY

The old paradigm for creating launch program ideas is essentially an exercise in trying to read the client's mind. If you are clairvoyant (or if your best friend works at the company and can whisper in your ear about whether the direction you are taking makes sense), you will develop a launch plan that is on point. If not, you've just wasted a lot of time, energy, and agency money.

Idea Camp™ Is Born

A decade ago, we decided to try something different, and lo and behold, it worked! We've been refining this new paradigm ever since.

> **"While you're always looking** for best practices, it's important to realize that there aren't any cookie-cutter approaches to launch. You can't approach each launch the same way; it all depends on the product, and you have to be savvy enough about the audience and what's the best way to reach them. It's about understanding the market your client is in and what's already out there and how you can play off that. If you're a consumer in that market, think about how you want to read about the product. If you're not in the market, find someone who is and get to know how they think."
>
> — *Hector Marinez, Vice President of Porter Novelli Bay Area, San Francisco, California*

Here are the basics of how our Idea Camp™ works:

We assemble the entire team (the client, ad agency, PR firm, other promotional partners, and target consumers) in the same room at the same time to brainstorm launch plan ideas. Our facilitated creative problem-solving process yields hundreds of potential ideas, which we vote on and evaluate as a group to determine which concepts meet program objectives. (One of the client executives serves as team captain to guide and make decisions when the group needs input from the top.)

Using the best ideas voted on by the group, we develop a launch plan that grows out of the ethos of the company. The ideas are appropriate only for this specific company, because they come directly from the team charged with bringing the product to market. The ideas respect the product, its brand, and the company's heritage. We've found that internal people can generate excellent external ideas. It's just that external consultants don't typically ask internal people to share their points of view during the launch plan development process.

Our experience shows that the best launch plans are developed by a healthy mix of internal people (including marketing, sales, R&D, operations, finance, and PR) as well as external consultants (advertising, PR, Web, promotions, and other agencies) and consumers of the potential product (whether they be adults, teenagers, or children). Using the concepts generated in Idea Camp as the basis for the launch plan, we are able to craft a strategy that speaks to both the brand image and the personality of the company *and* its new product.

We always ask ourselves, "This is such an effective methodology; why did we ever do it a different way?" Even today, many clients try to persuade us to eliminate Idea Camp and move straight to program development to save time and money. But whenever we capitulate to this demand, the campaign ends up weaker than the ones created using our proprietary process. Naturally, we're disappointed when a company decides it doesn't need this step and hires another agency that creates a plan without using a collaborative process (i.e., using the old paradigm described in the previous chapter). But it's our belief that if we skip team brainstorming, the launch will be compromised. Supporting this belief is our observation that when a company hires an agency to do a streamlined planning process, often the company is back on the street within months, initiating yet another agency search after a launch that didn't live up to expectations.

It's About Bonding

But Idea Camp is more than just ideation. It's a way to get the entire team to bond. The first step in getting team members to forge solid connections with each other takes place at the organization meeting described in Chapter 16. The ideation session builds on that foundation of camaraderie, joint purpose, and respect.

Why is bonding important? Because you want the marketing team to coalesce and support one another — and this happens only if everyone buys into the strategic direction of the launch. For a launch to be truly successful, a company needs a unified vision, and one thing we've learned about working with big companies is that unity is a rare thing. Once you add in all the competing agency partners, each with its own point of view and a vested interest in a bigger piece of the launch budget, you can see why reaching consensus is challenging. But having a unified theme or direction for a new product launch is critical. If everyone agrees to travel the same launch path, the product message will be extended across advertising, public relations, promotions, and the Internet, making success more attainable as all disciplines reinforce the same key message. It's difficult and expensive to build consumer awareness so having a strong single message across all marketing channels builds new product recognition and sales much faster.

Brainstorming Together Produces Great Results

Clients are thrilled with the ideas and camaraderie born in Idea Camp. For us, the process is far less agonizing and incredibly more rewarding than going it alone. And most importantly, the campaigns we develop in true unison with our clients tend to be extremely successful.

Towering Success

When we first started working with New England Confectionery Company (NECCO®), America's oldest multiline candy company,

we held an Idea Camp to galvanize the team and develop concepts to celebrate the company's 150th anniversary. Operating
under the theory that there are no bad ideas when brainstorming,
NECCO president Dominic Antonellis, a first-time participant in
Idea Camp, mentioned, "I have to paint the water tower that sits
on top of the factory, and right now the plan is to paint the tower
gray." This comment sparked a barrage of ideas that finally
resulted in the water tower being painted to look like the world's
largest roll of NECCO wafers. We then wrapped up the water
tower and unveiled it to signal the start of NECCO's 150th year in
business. The Schneider & Associates team crafted a yearlong
anniversary campaign that resonated with consumers and resulted in major placements, such as a four-minute piece on NBC-TV's
"The Today Show."

For NECCO's world-famous Sweethearts® Brand Conversation

Hearts, we hold an Idea Camp each year
right after Valentine's Day to begin thinking about the theme for the next year's
campaign, since it takes an entire year to
manufacture the more than 8 billion lit-
tle candies. Successful themes have featured supporting literacy
and education, empowering young women, helping arts and
design students with scholarships, and promoting the new mil-
lennium. In 2004, the U.S. Postal Service released a new love
stamp, the first redesign in many years. NECCO and the USPS
worked together to launch the stamp and the 2004 sayings at an
extensively covered press conference prior to Valentine's Day.

By creating an annual event that, in effect, relaunches the
Sweethearts Conversation Hearts every year, we've developed
an annuity for NECCO. Coverage for the press conference on the
new sayings often goes around the world (since NECCO does
not believe in video news releases, satellite media tours, or any
newfangled way to generate coverage, all national media we
obtain is from local affiliates feeding the story by satellite to the
national affiliates).

Going to Great Heights

When HP Hood in Chelsea, Massachusetts, approached us to
launch their new premium brand of ice cream, Peak Treasures, we

began the planning process with Idea Camp. The integrated team developed guerrilla marketing ideas to introduce the new product, which prominently featured a snow-covered mountain peak on its packaging. To honor the name and the iconography on the carton, we created a campaign focusing on events that used "peaks," or stressing that Peak Treasures was "tops." Designed to drive trial and purchase, these  Sneak "Peak" Events in five major New England cities included a mobile climbing wall for kids, stilt walkers, and lots of ice cream product sampling. (Note: When you're selling out-of-the-box-ideas, make sure you anticipate the factors that could tank your idea. We knew management would be concerned about the liability issues relating to kids using the climbing wall. For our presentation, we brought along an insurance expert who explained how each event could be easily covered with an additional rider policy.)

Another idea that came out of Idea Camp involved creating an enormous inflatable mountain to install on the HP Hood factory just prior to the July Fourth weekend; the factory is visible from major highways and commuter railways in Boston and is seen by every commuter coming into the city from the north. Little did we know that persuading Boston city officials to give us the go-ahead to erect an inflatable mountain would be so difficult (yet another reason to build lots of time into your launch plan!). Ultimately, we were able to scale the obstacles and put up a huge inflatable mountain reminiscent of the packaging, capturing the imagination of commuters and the media.

Key Ingredients of Success

While we are constantly refining the way we conduct Idea Camp, the key components that make the process a success have remained unchanged. Any form of structured creative problem solving will achieve the results you're looking for as long as you have the following ingredients:

- **CLIENT IN COMMAND** — On this creative voyage, one person has to serve as captain of the ship. We deputize one representative from the client to have the final word on which ideas will be selected for further development at the end of the day. We also designate one agency person to serve as navigator; this person works closely with the client representative to help him or her move smoothly through the process from start to finish.

When we conclude a session, we may have 300 ideas, so the group as a whole votes on which concepts they believe have the most potential to produce outstanding public relations launch results. Then the "client captain" chooses from this smaller group of concepts to decide which ones will be developed as part of the actual launch plan. (You'll find more details on this process in the next chapter.)

• **SKILLED FACILITATOR** — Having your session run by a professional who's experienced in facilitated creative problem solving will dramatically increase the quantity and quality of your ideas. Companies sometimes confuse the ability to run a good meeting with the ability to facilitate brainstorming. A trained creative problem-solving expert has learned proven processes for bringing forth creative solutions in a group setting, where the dynamics can sometimes be difficult because of company politics or other issues. Facilitation skills are crucial, and they're not the same as the skills needed to manage a large group meeting where creativity and ingenuity aren't critical. And yes, you do have to pay these people, but they're worth it!

A good facilitator builds team cohesion, keeps the group focused, runs the meeting effortlessly, and handles issues and conflicts as they arise. A good facilitator knows how to foster an atmosphere where people feel free to offer ideas that may sound outrageous at first but actually have real potential.

In addition, an experienced creative problem-solving facilitator knows how and when to push people to create truly breakthrough creative ideas. He or she knows how to motivate people to stretch and think of more and different ideas — and won't hesitate to do so.

When companies compromise, however, and use an in-house leader who is not a trained facilitator, the results are usually disastrous. It's very difficult for an in-house person to lead a group in creative problem solving. An in-house facilitator, for example, may hesitate to take a senior executive aside and tell him that he's killing potentially good ideas by making negative comments about them before they can be fully explored, or that he's hogging all the air time. If the idea of using one of your staff as the facilitator for a new product brainstorming session comes up, pull out your best negotiation skills to persuade the person forwarding the idea that objectivity is the key to success. Hiring a trained, impartial facilitator will improve the ideation process by 1,000 percent.

• **BRINGING THE OUTSIDE IN** — The wider you cast your net for people to include in the ideation session, the better the ideas will be. People who work inside a company, no matter how creative they are, see things from the company's point of view, particularly if they've worked there for a long time. So while they may know a lot about the product and the market, they are often hindered by that company bias — the party line, so to speak — toward the product and its potential. That's why it's imperative to bring in people from outside the company to get a fresh perspective. People from the ad agency or the promotional firm, sales representatives or brokers who sell the product, as well as industry experts and even actual consumers all make the ideation process more real and effective.

You'll find that people who are peripherally involved with the product often have fresher notions than the product development team because the product people have narrowed their focus. With only insiders present during ideation, it's difficult for even the most highly skilled facilitator to break through narrowly focused thinking.

But with the fresh perspective that comes from having a diverse group of people creating ideas, it's easier for internal people to get behind concepts that would usually be far beyond their realm of thinking. We frequently hear clients say, "Wow, we hadn't thought of that," despite the fact that the proposed idea makes perfect sense and is fairly obvious

Another important way to bring the outside point of view into

brainstorming is to conduct Internet research about recent promotional campaigns in your product category prior to Idea
Camp. That way, if someone falls in love with an idea at the
voting stage, the facilitator can point out that it's a great idea,
but Company Y has already done it.

Good Ideas from Outside and In

Here are two quick examples that show exactly how important it
can be to have a diverse group when you're brainstorming ideas.

If You Listen, the Customer Is Usually Right!

We were working with Morgan Memorial Goodwill Industries to
help the charity increase sales of used clothing at its retail stores in
Massachusetts. We invited two regular customers from their
Boston and Cape Cod stores to join us for Idea Camp.

One of the customers, who clothed her children primarily at
the Goodwill store, asked a simple question: "Why do you have
your sales at the end of the month when government assistance
checks come out at the beginning of the month?" Now there was
a just-do-it idea if ever we'd heard one! By simply changing the
sales cycle to match the time period when customers had money
in their pockets, Goodwill could instantly increase sales at no
additional cost.

Timing IS Everything

Here's an example of the value of having a wide range of internal
people at your brainstorming session. We were working with a
major pharmaceutical company to ideate about a new product that
had a small public relations budget and no advertising budget at
all. We learned from an external research and development consultant that various applications of the same technology were
being licensed to different companies.

The product that Schneider & Associates was launching had
an April lift-off date and a PR budget of $150,000. During the
brainstorming, one of the technology partners said, "I wish we

weren't introducing your product in April." "Why's that?" we asked. "Because Company X is coming out with a different product using the same technology two months earlier, with a $20 million advertising budget."

Company X was a major competitor, and based on the colleague's news, which he had picked up at a trade show, everyone in the room was truly stunned that we could be "scooped" by the competition. The decision was made to accelerate our client's launch to January to get the jump on the well-heeled competition. The lesson learned? Include technology people in the launch brainstorming (which is rarely done). Aside from knowing all the details about the product, technology types often have industry knowledge that marketing people aren't privy to because they travel in scientific, not marketing, circles.

• **CLEAR MISSION STATEMENT** — Every ideation session should start with a clear idea of what the group needs to accomplish. The mission statement can't be too broad, because unfocused mission statements lead to unproductive sessions. Instead, the mission statement needs to be narrow and focused so people can easily grasp the assignment for the day.

We develop our mission statements after doing research on the client company, the new product, and the target market. Then, in consultation with the leader of the client team, we write a clear statement that succinctly details the purpose of the ideation session.

Here's a recent Idea Camp mission statement for a product line extension that illustrates the characteristics of a good mission: "Build a PR campaign for a revered brand's line extension of products that increases sales and educates consumers about the brand's heritage." This mission clearly defines the objectives of the launch campaign. It focuses the group on developing public relations ideas instead of advertising or promotion concepts, and stresses that the brand's heritage should be a key element of the campaign. It also acknowledges that the purpose of the campaign is to drive sales; while this may seem like common sense, the fact is that most PR campaigns build awareness, not sales. Advertising and point-of-purchase promotions actually drive sales in most cases. So making this distinction in the mission statement — that we wanted ideas that would drive sales — was important. It told the people at the brainstorming sessions that they were going to have to stretch, since it's difficult to come up with PR ideas that will directly boost sales.

Here's another sample mission, for a totally new product that was a technological breakthrough: "Educate consumers about this new product's technological advantage and create supporting integrated marketing efforts to differentiate it from the competition." Just as this mission statement does, it's important to define your target audiences. In this case, that target was consumers, not the trade or business media. Audience definition keeps the ideation session from wandering. In effect, it also tells you what audiences you are not targeting, which is especially important at the end when it comes time to choose among the various ideas.

This mission statement also highlights the need to develop an integrated marketing effort, not just a PR campaign or an advertising campaign. It emphasizes the importance of making this new product stand out from the competition. By clearly articulating the goals for the session in the mission statement, we were able to develop many direct-comparison strategies that might not have emerged otherwise.

• **ADEQUATE TIME** — Developing great ideas takes time. We devote an entire day to Idea Camp, and we often find the very best ideas are the ones generated in the second half of the day, when people are really flexing their creative muscles. It's essential to allow enough time for people to become comfortable with one another and with the process. Shortchanging your brainstorming time will almost always result in shortchanging your launch strategy.

• **THE RIGHT SETTING** — Everyone knows that abandoning the office for a more casual setting without the distractions of day-to-day business is essential for a successful team planning session. It's particularly crucial when the whole purpose of your session is to be as creative as possible. Ground rules such as no cell phones, beepers, Blackberries, or watches have to be strictly enforced if people are going to keep focused on ideation. It's also important to make sure that all logistics, such as food and beverage deliveries, are well scheduled and that adequate supplies of paper, markers, and brain-teasing toys are already in the room. Nothing short-circuits creativity like constant interruptions to call support staff for forgotten items.

• **POST-EVENT DEBRIEF** — Anyone who has been through a good brainstorming session knows what it's like to leave a meeting bubbling with enthusiasm for the hundreds of creative ideas that were generated. Then, a few days later it hits you that the concepts aren't as fabulous as they seemed in the immediate afterglow of the meeting. It's always important to do a debrief a few days after the brainstorming to make sure the ideas chosen for further exploration hold up after you've slept on them for a few nights.

19

How to Choose from
So Many Ideas

f you've done a good job of assembling all the success factors covered in the previous chapter, you'll end up with a room whose walls are papered with ideas on dozens of flip-chart pages. (Remember to number the pages as you develop ideas so you can keep track of which ideas followed previous ones.) The next step is one of the most important parts of your brainstorming session — deciding which ideas will move forward and which will be left behind.

It's critical to show your courage here and select only ideas that are new or breakthrough. Stretch yourself and your company, because doing the same old thing is not going to create news or generate customer trial and repurchase. Resist ideas that are comfortable, that have been done before — even if they have a new twist.

As Sal Cataldi, head of Cataldi Public Relations, Inc., in New York City, put it: "A fresh idea makes all the difference. It 'emotionalizes' your brand to create the human connection, the commercial pheromone, that lies at the foundation of all press coverage and brand loyalty. Not to be undervalued is what a fresh idea gives agencies and clients: something interesting and fun to work on through the high-pressured weeks and months it takes to bring campaigns to full flight. The best 'big ideas' have very big wingspans — a message that can extend and power a broad range of marketing initiatives, from trade media and sales promotion to the Internet."

As you look at the whole range of ideas, almost inevitably themes will start to emerge. Use these themes to sort the ideas. In some cases, actual campaign themes won't be clear yet, but the various marketing concepts will be. For instance, some ideas might fit under the theme of consumer education campaigns, and others might be targeted to trade audiences. You can sort by theme, by audience, or by idea — whatever makes sense. The key is to create some order around the ideas to determine which ones meet your goals.

It's Time to Vote

As mentioned in the previous chapter, you should give the whole team a chance to vote on the entire range of ideas. We often divide the voting into two categories of ideas. There are the just-do-it ideas, meaning they are so obviously winners that you don't have to think twice about whether they're the right things to do. And there are the ideas that are very appealing but which require more research before you'll know whether they might work. Allow people to select five to 10 ideas for each category — the just-do-it ideas and the intriguing ideas — and have them put colored stickers next to the ideas for which they are voting. For instance, if there are 100 ideas, allow five votes per category; if there are 300 ideas, allow 10 votes per category. Also, give participants five bigger stickers they can use to vote for the overall best ideas. Of course, if you're looking for more concepts to work from, give the crowd more stickers so you'll have a wider range of ideas to evaluate.

After people vote, you'll want to reorganize the ideas so you can determine which ones are winners. The client team captain decides which themes he or she would like to see developed, and then the entire team starts ideating all over again! While it may seem that you've wrung every possible idea from the group, the act of sorting ideas into themes and then voting usually re-energizes everyone and helps them look at things in a new way. For instance, just coming up with labels for the different themes from the original brainstorming can prompt lots of new ideas. (And oddly enough, regular bathroom breaks seem to foster new ideas as well!)

Stretching Leads to Breakthrough, Which Leads to Success

Throughout both rounds of brainstorming and then during the actual voting, the facilitator should keep reminding people that this is the time to stretch for new and groundbreaking concepts. No one should worry about whether an idea will work or how much it will cost to execute. And everyone should keep in mind that some of the most successful concepts start out as ideas that sound totally absurd when first uttered. In fact, the chosen concepts will be thoroughly researched and tested, and what finally emerges as the actual launch concept may bear little resemblance to the initial idea. Encourage participants to think out of the box and to offer wacky ideas. In fact, the wackier the better!

One method we find effective is to break the group into twos and threes and have them write their ideas on a large sheet of paper, with plenty of room to doodle, draw diagrams, and connect ideas. We then have each of the groups present their five best ideas and discuss how they thought of the concepts. This methodology always prompts more ideas from the group, and it's a particularly good break from large group brainstorming.

Team Thinking Works

One strength of using a true team process for generating launch ideas is that even if the client team's leader is highly conservative or already presold on a particular idea, that person won't necessarily rule the day. If the boss's idea doesn't make the cut when the group votes on which ideas it likes best, it's pretty hard for the boss to overrule the entire group and its vision.

The same holds true for agencies. We have sometimes come to Idea Camp with a great direction that we think is definitely the way to go, only to discover the idea isn't popular with the group. Guess what? We have to get over it!

Home-grown Ideas Can Work

Given the assignment to come up with an exciting new way for CVS/pharmacy to launch new stores, for example, we went into the brainstorming session convinced that each new store should partner with a major health institution in its town — ideally the most prominent hospital — for its community relations program. Our first store openings were to be in the Washington, D.C./Baltimore, Maryland, area so we conducted research prior to the brainstorming session and decided a prestigious children's hospital in the area would be perfect.

But it became clear during the brainstorming that our client had a different idea. They believed that working with small community organizations located within one mile of each new store (which was their trading area for each store) would be highly effective. Initially, we thought this concept was a "snore." But the client team was so enthusiastic about the idea and it had so many votes, we were forced to look at it more closely and find a way to make it work.

And work it did! The grassroots approach suggested by the CVS team was such a success that we rolled it out in 50 markets across the United States as the company bought other drug store chains and converted them to CVS/pharmacy. Each time we implemented the program, we succeeded in generating strong publicity for the new store and built an instant positive reputation for CVS. As the company grew, supporting local communities through these grassroots events demonstrated CVS was a retailer that was committed to the well-being of the neighborhoods it serves.

This example illustrates how working together with the client

> **"When a launch is** working beautifully, you can't become complacent and think that every launch will be like this. It's not that easy anymore. You can't rest on your laurels. You have to be on the edge of your seat, ready to take it to the next level. We have to ask, 'What happens after this?' That has to become our mindset."
>
> — *Sheryl O'Loughlin,*
> *Chief Executive Officer of Clif Bar Inc.,*
> *Berkeley, California*

team is so much more effective than having the agency work alone. It's disappointing for both the client and the agency when ideas are put forth that aren't valued by the client team, which often happens when agencies and clients do their launch strategy thinking in separate silos. When launch campaigns are designed in concert, not only are they stronger, but they have a greater probability of success.

20

Developing the Launch Messages

Before we leave the start-up stage of launch development and move on to implementation, we'd be remiss if we didn't raise the subject of product positioning. A key question to ask before any launch is this: What is the product positioning going to be? The positioning statement serves as the platform from which all launch communications should emanate. This critical sentence or paragraph can influence the selection of strategies and tactics used by all the agencies to create the launch campaign.

As public relations professionals, we're used to the fact that usually the client and its advertising or branding agency have already established the positioning by the time we're on board.

> **"What you really want to do** with your product positioning is to construct something that creates a strong emotional bond because that will overcome strong existing relationships with existing products. If you can find a way to enter a consumer's heart, you will enter their pocketbook."
>
> — *Joe Grimaldi, Chief Executive Officer of Mullen Advertising Inc., Wenham, Massachusetts*

So, we decided to interview several positioning experts to learn more about the methods they use to create this critically important launch element. Next thing we knew, we were running into loads of brick walls. Most folks were willing to talk about the subject only in the very broadest of generalities; others didn't want to talk about it at all. Phrases like "proprietary process" and "trademarked methodology" kept creeping into the conversation. Product positioning, it seems, is the black box of launch. Clearly, the methods that ad agencies and branding firms use to develop product positioning fall in the if-we-tell-you-we'll-have-to-kill-you category.

Of course, all this secrecy is somewhat of a moot point because the gurus of positioning, Al Ries and Jack Trout, wrote the bible on the whole topic two decades ago. Anyone who wants to delve into it can pick up a copy of the 20th anniversary edition of the classic *Positioning: The Battle for Your Mind*, published in 2000, and learn more or less all there is to know.

> **"To define the benefit** of a new category of products or services, my counsel to clients has been based on an adaptation of Samuel Johnson's quote, 'Language is best served by shared experience.' I believe new product descriptions are best served by using the shared experiences of consumers who purchase similar products. Relating what your new product does better or differently than existing products quickly conveys how your offering fits into buyers' lives as well as what need it meets or problems it solves."
>
> — *Ted Jursek, founder of Naive Wisdom, PSF, Kansas City, Missouri*

But even though advertising and branding people resisted telling us how they create a great new product positioning, they didn't object to telling us about the mistakes they see others making. So what we're going to do here is offer insights we gleaned from our interviews and other sources about common product positioning mistakes. We feel confident that by steering clear of these potholes, you can create a product positioning statement that establishes the strong platform needed for a successful launch.

Positioning Bloopers

If you're not already familiar with Abraham Maslow's hierarchy of human needs, then embrace it fully as you develop your product positioning. Scott Bedbury, a Seattle brand consultant who previously held senior marketing positions at Starbucks and Nike, wrote in his book, *A New Brand World*, that "too many products are pushed at consumers through blunt and often clumsy appeals to only the most basic needs [i.e., physiological needs for shelter, food, clothing, etc.] ... A more skillfully marketed product will appeal to emotional states ranked higher on Maslow's scale of human needs. ..."[1]

Located above the physiological needs on Maslow's pyramid are safety and security, love and belonging, esteem, and self-actualization needs. Now, Maslow estimated that only 2 percent of people ever achieve self-actualization, so if you're going to appeal to an emotional need on this hierarchy as Bedbury suggests, then you're left with safety and security, love, belonging, and esteem. There's plenty of room in that group for a solid product positioning that speaks to people's emotions.

Seth Godin, author of numerous books on marketing including, most recently, *Free Prize Inside: The Next Big Marketing Idea*, described the relationship between product positioning and Maslow's hierarchy of needs this way: "People don't buy things because we need them; they buy them because we want them. People buy a new product because it makes them feel powerful, loved and secure. Some marketers understand that; others are under the delusion that they're meeting our needs."

On the other hand, "the biggest mistake I see people making regarding the positioning of their new products is that they're crafting a positioning that is based on better versus different," said John Parham, division president of Parham Santana, a branding agency in New York City. "The most effective marketers know you can pound someone over the head for a long time to get them to believe your product is better; people are more receptive to 'this is different.' The most effective marketers have carved out a unique point of view for themselves."

Justin Holloway, executive vice president and director of brand planning at Hill, Holliday, Connors, Cosmopulos Inc., one of the country's biggest ad agencies and part of Interpublic Group of Companies Inc., said the biggest mistake marketers make is overcomplicating the positioning statement. "They [clients] have a technically correct positioning that covers so many bases that it doesn't position a company at all."

People [i.e., clients] get stage fright, contends Holloway. "If the positioning is too definitive, they feel it doesn't give them much flexibility," he said. "Then they broaden it, and it is still fairly clear. But it gets so many riders and caveats; it is so correct and long that it doesn't say anything anymore."

For any brand, Holloway continued, positioning is a sacrifice: "You enter the positioning process by coming to grips with the truth about the brand. If you are positioned to be 'a,' you are not going to be positioned to be 'b.' By deciding to have a positioning in the first place, you trade in ubiquitous appeal in favor of intense but more select appeal." Once again, a positioning that tries to be all things to all people won't work.

In a similar vein comes this positioning advice from Kevin Winston, senior vice president of Porter Novelli in San Francisco, California: "A lot of companies with technology products don't understand that if you get out there and play the numbers game in terms of your product's performance capabilities, in a month's time a competitor is going to trump that. So if you try to hang your hat on performance numbers, you're missing the point. Consumers will get to a point where they're so confused they won't even listen any more. But they will remember if you've made a connection between your product and their lifestyle."

Another big positioning mistake, according to Skip Dampier, president and chief strategy officer at Ross Creative + Strategy in Peoria, Illinois, happens when "companies don't create a unique position; they just add to the clutter. They don't take time to understand what consumers are looking for and don't make it [the positioning] different and new. Consumers are really sharp about not trying every new thing that comes along unless it's different. A lot of marketers are fabricating positions; it's one thing to have a position, and it's another thing to have one that consumers really desire."

7 Ideas About Product Positioning

Based on his experience working in agencies and observing consumers, Justin Holloway offers this advice on product positioning:

1. Don't make the positioning long-winded or open to interpretation. If a positioning includes too many different attributes, the launch team members will pick the ones they like and go off and do what they want, because the positioning allows them too much freedom.

2. It's unwise to create a positioning statement that appeals to everyone. All too often, positioning statements are written by committee. Everyone gets in their points of view; people feel good about it, but the position isn't expressed meaningfully. If the positioning statement is too consensus driven, it won't have the unambiguous clarity it needs.

3. Jumping around is a common positioning sin. If a positioning doesn't fly within the first three months, it gets dumped and the client moves on to the next one. The most successful positionings are well thought out and consistently adhered to year after year.

4. Make your positioning phrases catchy but don't turn them into tag lines. Holloway said, "I make them short, snappy, and catchy. They have a certain rhythm to them so people can remember; you don't want them to be ponderous and dull. You don't want people to have to pull out a PowerPoint presentation to remember what the positioning is. Positioning statements must be memorable."

How is a positioning statement different from a tag line? There's lots of confusion about these two disciplines, and sometimes, in fact, the positioning line becomes the tag line. Cautioned Holloway: "It probably shouldn't; there is an ideal halfway house. You don't want to have a boring, long-winded positioning line, but if you get too cute, it can be the tag line, [and] that's not usually the right way to go."

5. You have to have discipline at the beginning of the process. You have to be tough. Clients will say, "I love it, but can we just get this phrase in?" A strong agency partner has to say, "No, we can substitute that phrase if the substitution is stronger, but we can't keep adding." All too often, people think the positioning is only words on a page, but every addition to those words weakens the whole statement.

6. Marketers don't want to leave it up to the consumer to discern the positioning; they want to serve it up. But the truth is, consumers won't accept the positioning if they don't come to it by themselves. You give them all the information, you lead them in the right direction, and then you let them make up their own minds. You can prod them along so they get it, but you can't spoon it down their throats.

7. Clients think they own their brand positioning, but in reality, the consumer owns it because it exists only in the mind of the consumer. You can blame no one but yourself if consumers don't understand the positioning the way you want them to.

The Imperative for Real Research

Finding out what consumers really want, of course, requires research. And this is where some marketers get into trouble developing not just their product positioning but also their entire launch strategy. "The difference between a really good marketer and a mediocre one is a well-developed gut," said Ted Seisser, chief creative officer of Saatchi and Saatchi in New York City. "They both get the same research, and the person with the well-developed gut will know when to go with the research and when to ignore it. You have to listen really hard to what the consumer is telling you about what they want, but don't over-research what you hear; go with your gut. It's not a matter of black and white; you need to read between the lines of the research."

Seisser said his agency's philosophy is to develop what they refer to as "love marks," which make the emotional connection with the consumer. "We're looking for a connection that garners loyalty beyond reason; that is the goal. With a new product, at the beginning of that process, we try to determine what is going to be the emotional trigger to get people to fall in love with it," he said.

Good research helps you understand what the market is asking for. Then you can decide whether your product meets that need, and if it doesn't, whether you can define a positioning that identifies a need people have but haven't yet recognized. Here's how Jeff Pacione, creative catalyst at Catapult Thinking, a Boston design innovation group that develops brand strategies, described what he and his colleagues try to accomplish in their research: "We seek to understand the customer journey. What is the total cycle of interaction that our customers have with the product? How much time do they spend on the buying decision? Who consults with them? How important is the price? What are the tangibles versus the intangibles that cause people to buy? We want to know every aspect of that process."

This type of in-depth consumer knowledge isn't easily gained from the traditional research standbys of focus groups (where you and your consumer are separated by a pane of glass), telephone surveys, and mall intercepts. As Seisser pointed out, "Consumers say what they think they should say. For instance, if you do research with women and talk about child nutrition, they will say they only feed their kids the best of this and the best of that. Meanwhile, sugar foods are flying off the shelves, and no one is admitting to it in structured research."

Once you accept that the old methods of research aren't providing you with solid, actionable information, you will quickly discover ways to get closer to real customers. For Old Mother Hubbard Dog and Cat Food, a Schneider client that Catapult Thinking shares, Catapult did a series of "dog intercepts" at places where people who have strong relationships with their pets hang out. "We talked with pet owners at independent pet stores, where consumers  are encouraged to bring their animals, at parks, dog runs, and just walking on the street. We wanted to understand the interaction between the consumer and his or her pet," explained Pacione. "We were looking for people who had a strong affinity with their pets and with the product. Those are the people who will be the bedrock on which the brand will grow, so understanding them is critical."

For Virginia-based Smithfield Foods Inc., Skip Dampier's agency recruited nine families that fit the company's audience profile. The women were given diaries for two weeks in which to write about topics such as grocery shopping, meal planning, cooking, and serving meals to their families, the family's media consumption, and dining out experiences. They also kept all their grocery receipts. Then the agency had each family invite a "friendship circle" over for an evening of food and drink, and the entire party served as a focus group.

"The fun thing," said Dampier, "is that we had them do a pre-survey about how many trips they typically made to the grocery store, how much was spent per visit, and how many stores they visited per week, and all of that information turned out to be different from what they actually did during the two weeks. So the insights we got were much more real and much deeper. These learnings will help us understand what's going on in people's minds and their unexpressed desires. We'll look at how we can help Smithfield overcome the dissonance in the market between what customers want and what its competitors are offering them. How do we create this little bit of magic here, and how do we link that emotional tug with our product? The positioning that comes out of that has to be believable and sustainable."

At Hill, Holliday, they use ethnography to get close to consumers. According to Holloway, "We spend time in homes with consumers observing how the brand or the product fits into their life rather than the artificial construct of them coming to a focus group. It's living with the consumer as they live with the brand. It's a much more contextual type of research that is also more motivationally based. It's going and watching people. Sometimes we watch them on camera or in person; we see firsthand how they interact with products."

Holloway continued, "We go into stores and watch people hang out. We see what questions are asked, learn how the purchase process works. Rather than relying on consumer' narrative or reportage, we go out and watch people buy brands and report back about what we see."

> "**Launch messaging should be** very feedback focused. Feedback is an interesting thing because on one hand, it's a great tool. You can learn as you go. But feedback also is one of the most effective forms of building advocacy. We're in an era where traditional advertising does not work, but when you ask someone their opinion in an interactive medium like the Internet, that's a way to hold their attention for a longer period of time and to show respect for your customer."
>
> — *Pete Blackshaw, Chief Marketing Officer of Intelliseek, Cincinnati, Ohio*

From Platform to Messaging

Believable and sustainable: Those are two words to live by when you're developing a product's positioning. But what do you do once you create a positioning that meets these criteria? How do you make sure it sets your new product apart from its competitors?

According to Joe Grimaldi, chief executive officer of Mullen Advertising in Wenham, Massachusetts, the positioning should be used to 1) define what you want the communication to do, 2) stimulate creativity in solutions development, and 3) evaluate the work that comes out of the creative teams.

In most organizations, refining the launch campaign from the positioning is an iterative process. You start off with a handful of ideas about how to execute the positioning. As you begin to formulate how these ideas would be executed in the various marketing disciplines, you start to get a sense of which ideas will work best in which medium. In each iterative round, you delve further into specific strategies and tactics and how they can be delivered across the different marketing platforms. Finally, you hit upon what will hopefully be the perfect launch concept — one that leverages the product positioning to its maximum and achieves that "believable and sustainable" goal mentioned earlier.

In marketing public relations, the key positioning-related tool we create for each launch campaign is the Media Message Guide. Essentially, the Media Message Guide is the platform for all communication with the media and other key audiences, whether that communication is in writing (the press kit or e-mail pitches) or oral (phone pitches, interviews, and follow-up). The Media Message Guide should drive what the company executives, the customer service people, and the sales team say about the launch. It is the bible when it comes to the approved messages the company wants to use for the product and the launch campaign.

After this important tool is in place, the actual writing of the press kit and other collateral pieces becomes fairly simple. The key messages have already been established, and much of the research and statistics that normally go into a press release or fact sheet have already been completed. The Media Message Guide also serves as a tool for training spokespeople for their interactions with the media and for public appearances.

Here are the basic components of a typical Media Message Guide:

1. SINGLE OVERRIDING COMMUNICATIONS MESSAGE: This should consist of one or two sentences that sum up the major points you want to communicate about the product. It is the one statement you want everyone to memorize and always use for the product.

2. SUPPORTING MESSAGES: These should reinforce the overriding message and provide additional information or proof points to solidify your credibility and tell the story. Again, the entire team must commit the supporting messages to memory. When combined with the single overriding communications message, these facts provide the "short story" you want to consistently tell about the product.

3. KEY WORDS: This list, preferably no longer than 10 words, includes the touchstone words used in the messages. By memorizing this short list, spokespeople and those who are pitching media stories have an easy way to remind themselves of the key messages. Be sure to include key words from the product positioning, such as the adjectives that bring the product to life and express the emotions you're trying to evoke. For example, the list of key words we developed for the launch of a bra for women with ample curves included curvaceous, vibrant, sensual, self-confident, and comfortable.

4. "DO NOT USE" WORDS (OPTIONAL): If there are words that are often mistakenly applied to your product, your brand, or your company, include those words here. Also list words that should not be used to describe your target market. To return to the example mentioned earlier, the do-not-use list we developed for the bra included words like full-figured, plus-sized, large, big, overweight, and heavyset.

5. KEY MESSAGES: Key messages are often broken into sections. For example, you might have a section for product and brand messages, a section for corporate messages, and a section for event/program messages (about your launch event and related programs such as contests). Each section should contain no more than six to 10 concise messages that make ample use of the key words. Be sure the messages are user-friendly and not written in stilted language. Avoid lingo at all costs. The messages must be easy and comfortable to deliver, and understandable to people who are not in your industry. Key messages should also be conversational and tested to ensure they are useable sound bites.

6. Q&A: This section should focus on commonly asked questions, including the ones you dread answering. In addition to the questions, include the recommended responses, again using key words and key messages. You might have two Q&As: one that gets included in the press kit and handles Frequently Asked Questions (FAQs), and another that articulates the answers to tough questions you hope never get asked (and certainly don't get circulated to the media). It's important to be familiar with how to answer both the slow pitch questions and the hardballs. We also recommend practicing the answers to all questions before every interview. In addition, the answers to certain questions may change over time. Be sure to update your Q&As and/or FAQs regularly.

7. FIRST/MILESTONES: If your product is breakthrough or is creating a new category or accomplishing some other first, this is the place to include that information. Also, if your company has achieved other firsts or significant milestones that help support your new product message, include those here as well.

8. ANALOGIES (OPTIONAL): If your product is difficult to understand, provide some useful analogies that can be offered to help support the key messages.

9. MYTHS & MISCONCEPTIONS (OPTIONAL): Oftentimes, you have to overcome either negative impressions or misconceptions about a product category, about the consumer problem your product addresses, or even about your consumers. For instance, in completing this section of the Media Message Guide for Dermaläge, a client that produces crèmes for menopausal women, we dispelled widely believed myths about the impact of menopause on women.

10. THIRD-PARTY ENDORSEMENTS: Third-party credibility is often critical to supporting your key messages. Members of the media frequently want people outside the company to quote about the efficacy of the product or the emerging trend into which the product fits. This section can contain brief (two to three sentences) third-party testimonials about the product or your company. Or, you can include a list of third-party contacts (with phone numbers) who will provide comments to the media. This list comes in handy during media interviews as a source sheet of experts you can suggest as ballast for the story.

11. INDUSTRY/TREND OVERVIEW/STATISTICS: Again, this is the type of information that reporters love. Keep it brief, with no more than six to 10 facts. You don't want to drown your spokes-people in data, so choose the really important information that you want them to remember and convey to the media. Also, you can always e-mail or snail mail additional facts to a reporter based on how an interview progresses. Follow-up is a good thing, and following up to provide pertinent facts is an excellent thing.

12. MAJOR COMPETITORS: In this section, you try to antici-pate questions about the competitive environment your new product is entering. The messages should offer a way to respond to an inquiry about the category and the overall mar-ket without dwelling on competitors. The goal here is for your spokespeople to fit the product and its launch quickly into con-text and then bring the focus back to your own key messages.

13. GLOSSARY OF TERMS (OPTIONAL): If your product is highly technical, a glossary of terms can be helpful in bringing your spokespeople and the media up to speed quickly. Remind your spokesperson to use everyday language and to avoid tech-nical jargon that consumers and the media might not under-stand. Clear, simple language is the best way to explain some-thing new.

Media Message Preparation

When you're developing a Media Message Guide, here are some important considerations to keep in mind:

- Messages need to be consistent, no matter which media audi-ence is being targeted. The trade and business media have dif-ferent interests than the consumer media, so you'll need to create messages specifically for each audience; different information may be emphasized with one group that is not important to another. Overall, key messages about the product should be consistent for all audiences.

• Message development requires a balancing act. This is a bigger issue for some product categories than for others. For anything being launched in the medical arena, for example, the message has to balance what the product research indicates, the claims you're going to make on the product labeling, and what your lawyers and government organizations like the FDA will allow you to say.

• Understand the difference between what you want to say and what the media will actually say. The ideal media message is one that meets as little resistance as possible from the media. In other words, the challenge is to create messages that can easily make it through the filter of the media and arrive at your target consumer with a minimum of media alteration or interpretation. This is not an easy thing to do, especially in today's jaded media environment where editors and reporters are highly skeptical of any new product claims. Obviously, knowing what messages will resonate with — instead of bouncing off — the media requires a thorough understanding of what your target media cover and what triggers their interest. (As an aside, maintaining relationships with reporters on a particular beat helps in this regard. All too many companies make the mistake of contacting the media only when they have a new product to tout. Then they wonder why their message doesn't move to the top of the reporter's list! Like all good things in life, relationships take time to cultivate.)

• Understand what kind of supporting information you need to provide to establish credibility. Just what this supporting information consists of depends on the type of product you're launching, the environment in which it's being launched, and the positioning of the product. For example, trying to launch an over-the-counter medical product without having recent clinical trial data to support your message about the product's efficacy is a challenge. Similarly, not having a third-party medical professional as a spokesperson adds to the difficulty of developing credible media messages for such products. In the event you don't have the research results or a third-party professional to serve as a spokesperson, but instead have consumers who love the product and are willing to talk about it, you may be able to bridge the gap by leveraging the power of consumer testimonials.

Products that don't yet have any distribution are of little interest to the media (unless they're coming from companies with proven track records). So if your messaging doesn't include information on distribution, it may be too early to start talking to the media. If you say your product is "national," then you have to be able to say where consumers can buy it across the United States; calling a launch "national" when it isn't will kill your credibility with the media. If your product is distributed only regionally, consider having a regional launch. The ace in the hole here is the global reach of the Internet. If your product is sold on your Web site or other Web sites, the media will accept that it is a national launch.

• Don't carve your messages in stone. You want to be able to take advantage of things you learn along the way as you move through your launch. Some media messages may be met with great skepticism by the media. Others may produce that worst of all responses — dead silence. Listen to feedback from important audiences. Learn as you go, and keep honing the messages so they provide clearer, more effective information. Then, be sure to edit the Media Message Guide, the press and collateral materials, as well as your Web site to reflect any substantive changes that you determine can impact your product's credibility or sales.

GETTING IT DONE:
LAUNCH TOOLS & TECHNIQUES

The quest for the ideal mix of launch tools and techniques is a lot more complex these days, thanks to media formats and launch platforms that weren't even dreamed of a decade ago. In this section, we look at tried and true launch tools, as well as some newer ways to interact with consumers and spread your launch message. We also tackle the complex issue of gaining distribution so people can find your product on store shelves after they hear about it. In addition, we offer ideas for targeting significant market segments, including mature adults, women, teens, and Hispanics.

21

GETTING IT ON THE SHELVES

As we discussed in Chapter 5, placing a new product on store shelves has never been more challenging. It's the old chicken and egg syndrome: If you don't have distribution, you can't prove the product will sell. If you don't have sales, you can't secure distribution. Couple this with the need for proving the efficacy of your product (such as clinical trials if it's a drug store product) or developing market research to show the product will motivate consumers to buy, and you're in a tough spot.

Here's where creativity comes into play. How do you get your product in the hands of your target consumers? Do you send the product to influencers and ask for feedback? Do you hand out samples on street

> **"Overcommitting is a big mistake.** You are so excited to get the sale when a retailer with 2,500 stores says, 'We want to take your product nationwide.' ... If you offer the product but can't deliver, undersupply and underperform, the likelihood the retailer will deal with you again is at risk."
>
> — *John Rattigan, Director of Marketing and Business Development for Colorado Boxed Beef Company, Auburndale, Florida*

corners and at public events? Do you develop distribution points at places that make sense? Do you try to sell it into smaller retailers, and then build a comprehensive marketing campaign in that market to prove the product moves? While there's no silver bullet, manufacturers and distributors of new products always need to have a Plan B — and maybe even a Plan C — in case Plan A, selling to the big retailers, takes longer than anticipated or doesn't happen at all.

Clearly, small manufacturers, especially start-ups, are at a big disadvantage when it comes to securing shelf space. Most of the companies we talked with that overcame the distribution hurdle did so by taking a start-small-and-build approach. They focused on a few smaller retailers and built credibility in regional markets before going after the retail giants whose slotting fees they couldn't afford initially. The other thing these scrappy, resourceful marketers have in common is that they used a pull strategy: Consumers started asking retailers to carry the product, adding critical leverage to the marketers' own efforts to get shelf space. The combination of these two strategies often resulted in significantly lower slotting fees; retailers were willing to negotiate when they could see a market for a product already existed.

Here are four examples of how this strategy worked for smaller companies:

- **JONES SODA:** "When we first launched Jones Soda, we didn't have the money to pay slotting fees," explained Jennifer Cue, chief financial officer and chief operating officer. "The most difficult thing in the beverage industry is to get distribution. You need good, solid distributors who will support the brand and are focused on it; if you don't have this, the brand will die no matter what you do. A lot of people won't take a risk on a new product. So we chose three cities where we opened up alternative accounts like tattoo parlors and skateboard shops; we purchased our own coolers and put them in the market. This gave us good marketing value, and putting our coolers and our brand in hot, hip retail outlets helped build demand. Then we convinced the distributors to take us on once we had a sales base. The word got out — people were asking various retailers to carry Jones Soda. We got into bigger accounts and weren't charged as high slotting fees because consumers were asking for the product. That helped us when we had little capital. Our alternative account strategy worked so well when we were launching a brand that this strategy became one of the pillars of our brand."

Today, Cue believes the lack of cash to support the initial launch was a blessing in disguise. "If we had had a big whack of money at the start, I sometimes think we would not have come up with such unique selling strategies. The alternative ones we used grounded the brand. The distribution strategies we used had authenticity; kids had time to discover the brand. It became their own brand because we didn't push it on them."

• **COCOA PETE'S CHOCOLATE ADVENTURES:** "Launch your product locally, take small steps, and get your product into people's mouths," is the advice of Pete Slosberg, chief executive officer and cofounder. After great success creating Pete's Wicked Ale, Slosberg launched a chocolate company dedicated to bringing high-quality chocolate to a broader market than most gourmet chocolates reach. "If you can prove what you are doing is different from everyone else, retailers will give you more shelf space," Slosberg said. "Sure, it's hard to get distribution, but if you can demonstrate you are in a growth category, your segment is on fire, and they can make more profit because of the higher dollar amount per ring on your item, you've got a case. Start through specialty doors and build one door at a time. They are always looking for new things, whereas big chains want to take your first-born."

Slosberg is a big believer in mingling in public with the new product, something he does regularly. "Rent a van, do sampling in stores, and forget about advertising at first. Hand your product out, talk to people, get them talking about you and your product," he advised. "Develop apostles, communicate with them, do education with them, tell them about changes in the company, answer all questions on the 800 number, give customers a live person to answer their questions. At our sampling tables, we have the 'Moan-o-Meter.' When people taste our chocolate, we register their moans on the 'Moan-o-Meter,' which always draws a crowd."

- **LUNA®:** When Clif Bar Inc. launched LUNA, a whole nutrition bar for women, they followed the practice the company always adopts with new products: "When we brought the product to retail, we kept it narrow and went only to certain types of  accounts. That slow-growth model allows us to be more careful with our investments so they pay back more quickly. Or, if it doesn't work, we can quickly pull the product and move on," said chief executive officer Sheryl O'Loughlin. "We already had support for Clif Bars, particularly in natural food stores, so we were a known entity to the trade. When LUNA started moving, the trade started paying attention. The consumer was pulling it through, so then the trade decided to be part of it in a bigger way. Having that strong consumer pull to encourage retailers to carry LUNA, to convince them that it has to be on the shelf, was important.

"Sales grew naturally, starting in natural food stores which, at that time, were willing to experiment with products. Soon, grocery accounts saw LUNA had so much potential that they decided to bring it on, and we didn't have to play slotting fees. As a small company, we literally couldn't pay slotting fees.

"The key thing we do here is that we know that financial investment is a powerful thing," added O'Loughlin. "It can be great, but it can be dangerous. We don't have lots of money to spend; we are privately held and must be careful about our resources." The company's philosophy is to invest in new products at low levels and let the marketplace decide if the product is going to make it.

"When the marketplace tells us we are going to make it, we spend more to support the product," explained O'Loughlin. "This allows us to be able to fail, and sometimes we will. Being able to fail allows us to be able to gain breakthroughs; this helps us to come out with great new products that consumers truly desire."

Clif Bar was in the unique position of having a head start on generating consumer demand for LUNA. The initial impetus for the product was the numerous calls the company received on its customer service line from women saying they wanted more varieties of bars. "We always have our ears to the ground," said O'Loughlin.

By listening carefully to consumers, the company was assured that once the product was developed, women would start asking retailers to carry it. To help get out the word, the company distributed LUNA at women-focused events, such as the Lilith Fair, a concert tour featuring women artists.

• **RMH FOODS:** Jon Rocke, president of RMH Foods, which produces prepared meats, is a firm believer in launching small and building. "To achieve success, you may have to bite off small chunks; you may have to start locally and move regionally and grow from there," he said. "We do targeted regional rollouts. We approach retailers who are not as dependent on slotting fees and who see the value of a consumer spend. They understand how that will bring people to the store. Once you get sales, you can go back to the others. You're in a position of strength. We don't have the dollars for slotting fees, but we are going to spend the money for product support and consumer marketing to drive people into the stores."

Realizing that consumer pull is critical, Rocke said: "If you want people to try your products, you have to take a unique consumer approach. You need to get your product into people's mouths in nontraditional areas. We are going where people are: gathering for sporting events, going to different types of venues. We are taking our product out of the supermarket demo experience and giving consumers a whole new experience. We want their trial to be different from traditional experiences. The mobile scenario that goes where the people are — that's the right trend."

These "think small" strategies are the antithesis of what many manufacturers try, said marketing author Seth Godin. "Marketers insist on going to mass market immediately and ignore the power of developing early adopters who help you push your product. Mr. Heinz, Mr. Procter, and Mr. Gamble never [went mass market immediately] when they got started," he pointed out. "They worked their way up."

Godin suggested using the Internet to launch products inexpensively. "You can talk to people without a filter. People will be listening," he said. "In the food business, manufacturers could make a deal with five gourmet stores and give the product to them for free; if it catches on, agree that they'll buy it going forward, and then you don't have to pay slotting fees."

Full-Court Sales Press Produces Stellar Results

Energy Brands, Inc. wanted to move its Glacéau Vitaminwater and Glacéau Smartwater onto shelves at larger California retailers. After succeeding in smaller venues, mostly natural specialty food stores, the Whitestone, New York, firm set the stage for broader product distribution by creating a home delivery service for celebrities in Los Angeles. The good news: This A-list crowd was talking up the product in both LA and San Francisco, and consumers were starting to demand the beverage. Energy Brands knew it had to do everything it could to get the product onto store shelves. The bad news: The company couldn't afford the ad campaign that most retailers require before they take on a new product.

Lacking deep pockets, Energy Brands decided to use its best resource: a dedicated group of employees who were passionate about the product. The solution: The Mike-Ro Classic, an all-hands-on-deck sales drive named after the company's executive vice president, Mike Repole, and its senior vice president of marketing, Rohan Oza. After six months of planning, the company's sales force plus everyone in the corporate office — from the receptionist to the CEO — met in California for a full-frontal assault on the LA and San Francisco markets. In all, more than 100 people participated in the marketing blitz.

The company divided into two competing teams: Mike Repole's Greyhounds, who headed to San Francisco, and Rohan Oza's LA Ro-dawgs, who took on the LA market. Everyone spent a week going from store to store selling products. They opened up hundreds of new accounts and sold in thousands and thousands of cases. Samplings were naturally part of the effort; employees pounded the pavement, sharing their product and their passion for the brand and establishing new apostles.

Other strategies including placing an exclusive story with a leading trade publication, Stagnito Communications' *Beverage Industry*, which produced a cover story on the California marketing effort. Energy Brands brought the key reporter covering the story to California to spend a day experiencing firsthand what the launch and the brand were all about. Smaller stories were also pitched to other trade publications, which helped with retailer sell-in.

As a result of this effort, the company's California market doubled in the year after the Mike-Ro Classic, and the product enjoys in-store availability across the state. Similar campaigns were deployed in other markets, including Chicago, Illinois, and Miami, Florida, resulting in tremendously increased market share. Best of all, the entire company participated hands on in the company's growth and future success.

Be Realistic/Be Creative

As with any business relationship, understanding the challenges that your counterparts — in this case, retailers — are facing is critical to solving the shelf-space conundrum. "There's a reason retailers ask for slotting fees," said Eric Baty, chief operating officer of Brazilian coffee company Café Bom Dia, and formerly executive director of Consolidated Sales Network, an alliance of independent consumer product brokers across the United States. "They see so many ideas every day. They are selling shelf space; in fact, they

"**Don't depend solely on wholesalers** to sell in your product. Unless you have a physical presence, meaning your salespeople go out with the reps, they forget about you. The best thing is to have your own reps, because wholesalers are contracting and their portfolio of products is getting bigger and bigger. As a start-up with a few products, you don't get any mind share; they are selling the well-established products first because they know they sell. Make sure you have a presence with your wholesaler and key retailers… do whatever you can do to stay in touch."

— *Pete Slosberg, Founder of Pete's Brewing Company and Cocoa Pete's Chocolate Adventures, Campbell, California* are really selling real estate. Slotting fees are a left-handed form of insurance. If the product fails, the retailers get some recovery on the margin for what they took out of that slot to put the new product in its place.

"If manufacturers think they have problems, [they should] talk to the retailers," Baty continued. "They own the end product, and it's tying up their shelf space if it's not turning over. They have to be right about their decisions, as it is using capacity that could be sold to another product that might be more profitable. They're only making 2 percent pretax profit, they are publicly traded, and the pressure is on. They can't afford to be wrong."

In Baty's opinion, "too many manufacturers fall in love with what they are doing, rather than being stoic about what needs to be done. After all, there is only so much footprint available in CVS. If you are looking at distribution systems, don't just look at the retailer. Look at what you can do as the manufacturer that will create rapid or intense consumption. What kind of business model will provide high-velocity consumption? When the product you are selling is what consumers want, you don't have to worry about getting retailers to carry it."

Five Old Companies Learn a New Trick

In 1999, five of the nation's oldest privately owned candy companies formed the Candy Alliance, LLC, to improve their collective ability to compete with the confectionary giants. The participating companies — American Licorice Company, Ferrara Pan Candy Company, New England Confectionery Company (NECCO), R.M. Palmer Company, and Spangler Candy Company — reasoned that by working together, they could wield the purchasing power and marketing muscle that larger companies enjoy. They also hoped to boost their share of shelf space in the nation's mass retailers.

In less than five years, the Candy Alliance has tasted sweet success, signing a licensing agreement that names the consortium as the sales and marketing company for Disney confectionery products. The venture, which will operate under the name Imagination Confections, has untold potential value because the agreement covers virtually all ready-to-eat chocolate and nonchocolate confectionery items featuring Disney characters for food, drug, mass, convenience, military, vending, specialty, theater, video, dollar, and club stores.

"When we started the Candy Alliance," said Domenic Antonellis, president and chief executive of NECCO, one of the five partners in the alliance, "we asked, 'How can we put five companies together and take advantage of operating as one entity?' This enables us to combine our buying power to get better prices.

"For example, the Candy Alliance shares ads in *Nickelodeon* and *Disney for Kids*; every page is $25,000, and we are able to take advantage of combination packages that provide value-added for each company. In addition, we purchase shared trade advertising space to stretch our marketing dollars.

Antonellis continued, "We also buy IRI and ACNielsen marketing data together, which none of these companies could afford to get on its own. We also group our raw materials purchases, which provides substantial savings."

After its initial success, the Candy Alliance moved into the marketing arena. "Target was the first mass retailer who bought into the idea," reported Antonellis. "For example, we did a Halloween package where we all put products together, ship them as one invoice, and it all comes through one company. Buyers know who the five companies are — we're five of the oldest companies around. We divide the mass retailer customers and now call on them as a single source. NECCO calls on Wal-Mart, for example, and Spangler Candy Company calls on Target. That way, we don't have to call on all the companies as individual companies, and these buyers don't have to see five different people from five different companies. They see one senior person who represents all of us."

Could small companies in other sectors take a page from the Candy Alliance playbook in their fight for shelf space? Clearly, the advantages these five companies have gained in a relatively short period of time make the consortium idea worthy of exploration. Let's face it — not all companies can make the leap to working with their competitors. But when senior management is open-minded enough to embrace cooperation instead of competition, the resulting alliances can yield incredible financial results. The next time you're shopping at CVS or Wal-Mart and you see the Imagination Confections logo, remember that these five companies were major competitors who had the foresight to see that their future ROI was dependent on joining forces. Whom might your next partner be?

22

THE MEDIA DANCE

Time after time in our research for this book, people confirmed a key finding we'd learned from our own experience: There is no magic formula for launch. Marina Maher, founder of Marina Maher Communications, a New York City PR and corporate communications firm, put it best: "In 20 years in the public relations business, I have learned there's only one formula that works: Throw out the formulas! Beyond defining goals and objectives, all launches are individual. Having launched more than 100 products, I can tell you that there are similarities, but no two are ever exactly alike."

This reality means it's impossible for us to prescribe the ideal mix of tools and techniques you'll need to craft your integrated launch campaign. Bringing the creative ideas

"**Particularly in the tech area**, it's important to have visuals as part of your press materials. Reporters are hungry to see anything they can, but e-mail attachments get cumbersome. If you can set up a link to a Web site in the e-mail, that often works best."

— *Cori Barrett, Account Director for Access Communications, San Francisco, California* developed in your brainstorming session to life depends on a complex set of internal and external factors, some of which you can control and some of which you cannot. So, with one-size-fits-all solutions out the window, we'll look at a potpourri of launch tools, leaving it up to you and your team to select the most effective ones for your specific launch situation and objectives.

Publicity in the Driver's Seat

According to a 2004 Yankelovich study, 60 percent of consumers have a much more negative opinion about marketing and advertising now than they did a few years ago; 61 percent feel the amount of marketing and advertising is out of control, and 65 percent feel constantly bombarded by too much marketing and advertising.[1] Equally troubling is an Internet poll conducted by Forrester Research and Intelliseek that found only 24 percent of respondents agreed with the statement "Companies generally tell the truth in ads."[2] In this climate, publicity is increasingly likely to become the launch driver as consumers become more and more dissatisfied with advertising and other forms of marketing that they consider irrelevant, intrusive, or contrived. As we discussed in Chapter 12, "Don't Forget PR" is number 10 among the Launch Strategies suggested by the Schneider/Boston University research.

> **"PR firms don't give us enough** product information. They don't send photos, and they don't send nutritional information for food products. They don't send a sample or don't tell us what the distribution, retail price, and sizes are going to be. Don't send us four-page press releases: Use one-page releases and a list of bullet points. Don't send us sell sheets. When editors ask for information, they don't mean a sell sheet. Make sure you have photos."
>
> —*Jill Bruss, Editor,* PLBuyer,
> *Deerfield, Illinois*

Of course, the news potential of a new product varies from launch to launch. The weaker your news, the more creative your launch plan must be. The stronger your news, the more likely you can introduce the product solely on its own merits. Remember, the media are the final arbiters of whether your launch message goes public, and this is one jaded group of reviewers. Take a good hard look at the newsworthiness of your new product, and plan and budget accordingly.

If your new product is in either the me-too or line extension category, remember the advice offered in the Product Innovation Spectrum graphic in Chapter 10. It may be time to bring on the celebrities or to use cause-related marketing or sponsorships to generate interest, so you can create a launch story with more potential. Another possibility is to make the launch program itself the news. If you develop an inventive campaign or an initiative that is ultraunusual, you can tap into the increasing amount of media coverage that marketing campaigns are garnering. Considering how much consumers say they dislike being pummeled by advertising and marketing, it's rather ironic that there's such interest in news articles about these topics, but you might as well take advantage of it! Since a growing group of consumers closely follows news about advertising and marketing, leverage the situation by creating a unique launch strategy that generates interest in the new product by drawing attention to the campaign itself.

> **"Use two different press releases**, one for the trade and one for consumer media. The trade press is not the poor relative in the launch equation and shouldn't be treated that way. The trade press wants information like what sizes the product will be available in, the suggested retail price, and who is distributing the product. Understand the timing for the various media; trade publications in the food arena should have your news three months before the product arrives at retail. For daily newspapers, food editors work three to four weeks ahead, so you need to send them information four to six weeks before your product hits the shelf."
>
> — *Sarah Theodore, Editor,*
> Beverage Industry, *Deerfield, Illinois*

For example, as part of BMW's relaunch of the MINI Cooper in North America, the 12-foot cars were hoisted atop SUVs and then driven around major cities. This effectively made the point that MINI Coopers offer maximum utility at half the size of an SUV. Life-size fiberglass models of the diminutive cars, equipped with working headlights and taillights, mirrors, and other accessories, adorned billboards. The result: a flood of media coverage. Who could resist putting these visuals on the nightly newscast or in the newspaper? More important, the MINI enjoyed major first-year U.S. sales, exceeding expectations by 50 percent without the heavy TV ad budget of most new car launches.

What *Do* Reporters Want?

Here's media advice from Jennifer Barrett, an associate editor at *Newsweek* who regularly covers new products.

Q: WHAT ATTRACTS MEDIA INTEREST?

A: In general, new products that are innovative and that capitalize on current consumer trends tend to attract the most media interest. When I'm deciding whether to write about a new product, I usually ask myself four questions:

1. Does this product do something that is new and innovative?

2. Does it make our lives simpler or more enjoyable?

3. Does it empower its users?

4. Does it tie in with current trends (not fads) in the way people eat, work, travel, exercise, etc., that we've either recently reported on or plan to report on?

If the product doesn't answer these four questions to my satisfaction, I don't write about it.

Q: WHAT PRACTICAL ADVICE DO YOU HAVE FOR A BRAND OR MARKETING MANAGER?

A: When you're pitching your product to the media, it's important to highlight what is new about this product — why we should care or write about it. And just as important, why should we write about it now? The fact that your company has a new product is usually not in itself a story (unless you are a well-established company with a reputation for innovative and newsworthy products like Apple, for example, or Pixar Animation Studios).

You need to convince us that this new product will either change our lives in some dramatic way (e.g., a new line of low-carb foods, or cell phones that double as digital cameras), or that it has found a way to do something much more effectively than other companies are doing it (e.g., Google).

Strategies Worth Considering

Choosing the right media strategy is critical. Here are some approaches to consider:

- **GET KEYSTONE PLACEMENTS:** In *The Fall of Advertising & the Rise of PR*, Al Ries and Laura Ries talk about the importance of getting a "keystone" placement for your launch. That means placing an exclusive story in a venue so prominent that plenty of consumers see it, and other members of the media take notice and decide they have to cover your story too.

We like *USA Today*, *The New York Times*, and *The Wall Street Journal* for keystone placements. Editors, businesspeople, and the television assignment editors all read these publications religiously. If you announce something really new as an exclusive in any of these papers, rest assured the news will hit many other media outlets later the same day.

A perfect example of a keystone placement comes from McGrath/Power Public Relations, Santa Clara, California, which presented "Personal Technology" columnist Walter Mossberg of *The Wall Street Journal* with a MailStation to give to his mother. The pitch was that this product, an e-mail tool for people who are computer averse, was so simple that even Mossberg's mother would soon be sending him e-mail. The

> **"Some companies go into** a new product launch with the assumption that the fact they have something new makes it newsworthy. But nothing is newsworthy until you make it newsworthy by tying it into a trend."
>
> — *Sal Cataldi, President and Creative Director of Cataldi PR, New York, New York*

product worked as promised, and Mossberg wrote an effusive review. Done on a shoestring budget, the placement worked particularly well because in addition to showcasing the product, it also illustrated the typical buying scenario; many MailStations were purchased by adult children to give to parents who weren't computer users. And it worked! Sales shot off the chart, and even Al Gore's secretary called with his credit card number to order a MailStation for the then-vice president's mom.

To be efficient with this strategy, you need to consider, as Al Ries pointed out, "which publications want new ideas and which publications will run stories only after they have gained credibility in other media." No use wasting time on a pitch for keystone placement in a publication that only follows and never leads.

- **GO PUBLIC BEFORE THE PRODUCT IS SET:** Many companies are reluctant to do this, but telling the media about your new product before it hits the shelves can be appropriate in some situations. Again, Al Ries is a big believer in this strategy: "You launch the PR before the product is fixed," he told us. "The notion is to start early. The problem with most clients is they'll say we can't launch the PR before we know what we're going to charge for this or the features, etc. But there is always a reporter out there who wants to scoop somebody else, and if a product is not yet available for sale, you can make that happen. But if you wait to offer an exclusive until the product is in stores, it's too late. The product is out there for everyone — including reporters — to see. So you give someone a scoop *before* the product is on sale, and it goes from the Internet to trade magazines to general magazines. All of that takes time, so you have to start early."

Of course, this strategy is more feasible if your company has a reputation for innovation. The Gillette Company, for example, is able to use a "two-peak" media announcement strategy. It does an event to announce a major product three to six months before the product goes on the shelf, and then it does another consumer media push when the product hits the stores.

"Immediately after telling the sales force, we do a launch press event," said Eric Kraus, vice president of corporate communications at Gillette. "This is a business environment; it is a business story. There is no consumer angle except to seed interest. I want to control the dialogue about the new product, and the only way to do that is to announce it to the world. Now there is no chance there will be a leak, because we announced the news ourselves.

"At the same time, we hit the long-lead publications, which are usually three to four months out," Kraus added. "When their books hit, we want to be sure they have all the materials they need to run the story at launch time. The second peak is when the product is available at retail, and that's geared to the consumer press."

- **INCORPORATE STORYTELLING:** Storytelling is increasingly a part of marketing for many companies, and there's no reason it can't be effective for the media too. With the popularity of hip-hop and rap music, which are narrative driven, it's natural to build a story around your new product that can be used in packaging, point of sale, advertising, and events. Now take that one step further and move the narrative into the media relations portion of your launch program.

The MailStation story described earlier showed how this can work. Getting columnist Walter Mossberg to use the product with his mom produced a storyline with a broad emotional appeal that wouldn't have happened if they had just sent him the product and asked him to use it himself.

As Rolf Jensen, head of Denmark's Copenhagen Institute for Future Studies, explained, "As information and intelligence become the domain of computers, society will place more value on the one human ability that cannot be automated: emotion. Imagination, myth, ritual — the language of emotion — will affect everything from our purchasing decisions to how well we work with others. Companies will thrive on the basis of their stories and myths. Companies will need to understand their products are less important than their stories."[3]

As pointed out in *Trading Up: The New American Luxury*, a storytelling strategy might be particularly effective in attracting the so-called New Luxury consumers, the mass market segment that willingly pays a premium for selected product categories. Wrote authors Michael Silverstein and Neil Fiske: "New Luxury consumers also like to learn about specific products and the companies that make them. That's why so many New Luxury brands have a narrative associated with them."[4]

• **USE CONTROVERSY TO SELL:** Controversy as a media strategy isn't for everyone, but when it works, it really works. Just ask Mel Gibson as he counts the megamillions in ticket sales for his movie *The Passion of the Christ*. You might call it a throwback to the any-publicity-is-good-publicity days of yore.

Al Ries is an evangelist for generating controversy. "You have to build controversy into the product," he told us. "Every new brand that wants to be a success needs to have a controversy angle, and that will overcome the issue of not wanting to write about it. The thing that made *The Passion of the Christ* is the controversy."

Indeed, some commentators believe that a year before the film hit theaters, Mel Gibson deliberately set out to stir up a storm of red-hot publicity. *Boston Globe* columnist Alex Beam chronicled the path Gibson took beginning in January 2003, while the movie was still being made, to build an image of a highly controversial film. Beam dubbed the whole affair the "Christ con" and said it was the "most successful — and most cynical — movie promotion campaign in Hollywood history."[5]

Whether that's accurate or not, the point is that in some cases, generating media controversy around a new product can be extremely effective. As Al Ries told us, the original title he and his daughter, Laura, had selected for *The Fall of Advertising & the Rise of PR* was *The PR Era*. "But there was no controversy with that," he said, "so we changed the title, and that made all the difference in the world."

Companies often try to avoid controversy at all costs, asking, "Why would we want to make trouble for ourselves?" But controversy doesn't always mean trouble — it means creating a news edge that makes a story compelling. Engaging in a bit of competitive controversy can turn a launch that lacks a big news hook into a story that pits one major competitor against another. Provided that your part of the story has strong, positive messages, it might be worth the risk.

• **CASE IN POINT:** Honey Dew Donuts®, a New England coffee and donut shop chain, was a distant second to category leader Dunkin' Donuts. The two companies, both homegrown in Massachusetts, faced heated competition from Krispy Kreme, which was entering the New England market for the first time, and Starbucks, which was expanding rapidly in the region. To launch the yearlong celebration of Honey Dew Donuts' 30th anniversary, Schneider & Associates positioned the chain as the David against the big Goliaths. Sure, Honey Dew Donuts might get less ink compared with Dunkin' Donuts or Starbucks, but our main goal was to introduce the regional media to Honey Dew Donuts and establish the chain as a key industry player in the regional coffee-and-donut wars. The fact was, this chain had competed successfully against major competitors for 30 years and managed to grow to more than 150 stores.

Our "risk" strategy paid off. Virtually every major daily and weekly newspaper in Honey Dew Donuts' trading area ran a positive story about the company and its ability to survive and thrive for 30 years in an extremely competitive environment of distinct coffee flavor profiles. And, in a recent *Boston Globe* article about the "Coffee Wars," Honey Dew Donuts was featured as one of the major coffee forces in the Boston and New England area. This was the first time in 30 years that Honey Dew Donuts was positioned in the same story as Dunkin' Donuts, the 800-pound gorilla of the industry. The placement paid tribute to the importance of telling your story in a provocative — even controversial — way, which can generate awareness even if you aren't number one in the marketplace.

Is the Message Right?

In a tight economy, one of the first places the budget hatchet hits is the pilot programs that test whether launch messages resonate with target consumers. Carey Earle, chief executive officer of Harvest Communications in New York City, is a strong believer in testing not just launch messaging but also back-end operations to make sure everything is in place to support a launch.

Here's how she describes the challenges involved in persuading clients that this type of testing is important: "Unfortunately, in the economic environment we've been in for the last four or five years, marketers are so afraid to make mistakes that they keep doing things the same way they've always done them. Even if consumers tell them how they want to be communicated with, people are afraid to change what they're doing. They feel vulnerable to that one person above them who may question their choice. When people are operating out of fear, we have a hard time convincing them to pilot a program. Another thing that happens is companies are so wrapped up in hitting the launch date that the deadline becomes more important than having the right message."

Here's an example from Earle of the vital learning that can occur when launch messages are put to the test with real-life consumers: "We were working with one of the world's largest financial services firms, which was testing the concept and marketing of a new payment technology. As is true of any launch involving new technology, the challenge was whether people would understand it. The client thought the technology was so cutting edge that it was important to talk about [it]. In the first phase of a three-part pilot, various messages were tested with consumers. It became obvious the explanation of the back-end technology was confusing to people, and besides, they didn't even care about it! They simply didn't want to know how it worked.

"In the second phase of the pilot," Earle added, "the message focused on the simple three-step process for using the technology. We found that if we described five steps instead of three steps, people shut down. In the end, we didn't play up the technology beyond saying it was state-of-the-art. Consumers wanted the message to be as simple as possible, and the more visual the communication was, the better. What was interesting was that if we hadn't done the pilot, the client would have focused on the technology — instead of the benefits that the customers cared about."

> **"Don't give us a phone contact number** for someone who can't tell us about the product. We get press releases that have the administrative assistant's contact number; provide the phone number of someone who can answer our product questions. And don't make us chase them down."
>
> — *Nick Roskelly, Managing Editor, Stagnito's New Products Magazine, Deerfield, Illinois*

Test Back-End Operations Too

Earle also pointed out the importance of being sure that back-end operations work before launching a new customer service program or product. "Many companies spend a significant amount of money on a new customer program," she said, "only to get failing marks once the product hits the marketplace. To improve your success rate, conduct a pilot with employees at least three months before testing the program externally. This tactic builds employee morale and can help iron out some of the more obvious wrinkles before going to external markets. Once it's tweaked based on employee feedback, take the pilot to multiple external markets and test there for three months. Let the pilot participants know this is a test run. When audiences know it's a dress rehearsal, they tend to be more forgiving when sharing their dislikes or the problems they encounter. Test audiences also get a morale boost when they get to act as 'experts' whose opinions matter."

23

HOT ITEMS IN YOUR LAUNCH TOOL KIT

While **you definitely *don't*** want your entire choice of launch tools to be dictated by what's hot and what's not, you *do* want to keep abreast of effective new techniques. You also want to stay alert for improvements and updates to time-tested launch tools. With both those objectives in mind, here's a look at some new developments in the world of launch.

Word of Mouth

Results of the Schneider/Stagnito Most Memorable New Product Launch of 2003 survey confirmed that word of mouth has never been more important to new product success. More consumers in our survey learned about new products from family and friend recommendations than through any other avenue, including advertising. Some 55 percent cited these personal recommendations, while 53 percent cited television advertising and 48 percent cited in-store advertising and displays. Seventy percent of those surveyed said they recommend new products to friends.

Here's another reason that developing effective ways to build word of mouth for your new product is more powerful — and more essential — than it was even 10 years ago. As reported by consultants from Cambridge, Massachusetts-based Arthur D. Little, "In 1990, people regularly communicated with 50 to 100 people thanks to fixed telephony. In 2000, people regularly communicated with 100 to 300 people thanks to fixed and mobile telephony and the Internet. The value of individual communication networks has multiplied by ten in only ten years due to an increasing number of interactions offered by new communication technologies."[1] These figures show why viral marketing via the Internet has worked so well for some companies.

Clearly, leveraging today's robust communication networks can help you generate more word-of-mouth power than ever before. Most companies start this process by putting their new products and their launch messages in front of the so-called influentials — opinion leaders, trendsetters, innovators, and first-users who are most effective at generating person-to-person buzz. So prominent has the use of influentials become in marketing that New York City-based Ketchum, one of the world's largest PR firms, has created an Influencer Relationship Management Program to measure the impact of key people or groups that affect buying behavior. According to *Brandweek*, the program "reaches beyond the media, government and analyst types that are typically solicited to supplement a marketing campaign by identifying entertainment, authors, lifestyle leaders and others whose opinions are valued by consumers. Ketchum gauges an Influencer's attitude toward the client's position, which in part determines their effectiveness on consumers as measured by benchmarks such as recognition, endorsement and media quotes."[2]

While the number of programs geared to getting new products in front of influentials has grown, the techniques used are fairly simple, although often labor intensive. "We want buzz to be created," said The Gillette Company's Eric Kraus. "We constantly update the list of influencers and go to them ahead of the launch. We do VIP mailings two weeks before launch. We want opinion

> **"Too often people dumb** the launch down to just publicity. What is the goal? Possibly it's to win friends among key retailers. Look for something unusual. Demonstrate an attribute of the product in a creative way. Be able to stop people while they're page flipping. Viral marketing opportunities, advocacy, get people talking about it. These are the truly efficient strategies."
>
> — *Joel Curran, Managing Director of CKPR, Chicago, Illinois*

leaders, sports stars, entertainers, talk show hosts, and rock stars to try our new product. We get anchors on TV and radio stations trying the product ahead of time so they are talking about it. When it comes to new product launch, I am a huge believer in sweat equity. You have to do these basics extremely well."

As you consider developing an influentials-driven strategy for your launch, don't forget the important point that Ed Keller and Jon Berry of RoperASW make in their book, *The Influentials.* Influentials are not limited to the celebrity crowd. One in 10 Americans is an influential, and that adds up to 2.1 million people! These are the folks who in some way influence our thinking on a wide range of topics, including what new products to buy. Keller and Berry offer plenty of advice on how to develop a winning strategy for getting your message in front of the influencers in your target consumer group.

> **"I recommend the** marketing-the-marketing tactic. Consumers are very media and marketing savvy. When launching a new product, there is often an opportunity to communicate how you are marketing the product differently and get additional media exposure and buzz about the campaign, which leads to press about the product or service."
>
> — *Scott Russell, Chief Marketing Officer of MRA Group, Syracuse, New York, and Philadelphia, Pennsylvania*

Blogs and Other Internet Strategies

Of course, no communications tool can generate and spread word-of-mouth buzz faster than the Internet. Viral marketing campaigns that use the power of networks to speed word of mouth have proven very successful when carefully done. What Pete Blackshaw of Intelliseek calls "consumer generated media" is also proving to be highly effective in helping companies launch new products as well as tracking consumer impressions of existing products. From blogs to Web sites such as www.planetfeedback.com, where consumers rate products and share their opinions, people are chatting up a storm about what they like and dislike about products. Listening to this conversation is important for any company that values its customers' opinions, but actively participating in the conversation can also be an effective launch technique. Because information spreads so quickly via these methods, it's important to monitor the Web so you know what people are saying about your product. It's great to be in the discussion, but it's important to know whether the discussion is positive. And if the discussion is negative, it's equally important to work hard and fast to correct misconceptions or product problems.

For instance, Keri Bertolino, account manager of fama PR in Cambridge, Massachusetts, recommended: "Select bloggers with whom your company has some type of existing connection. Offer to give them a 'sneak peak' at a new product or service, asking for thoughts on your strategy, future direction, etc."[3] As Bertolino noted, however, it's important to be aware of the culture of the blogger community. They "own" their space and may resist what they view as efforts to manipulate it. Be smart and build a relationship first before you start pitching your new product.

On another Internet front, more consumer packaged goods companies are successfully drawing customers to their Web sites for product information these days. *The New York Times* reported that in July 2003, the top 10 sites for food and beverage makers attracted a total of 9.5 million visitors, up from just 5.4 million visitors in July 2002.[4] Product locator functions, which are especially effective for products sold only in specialty stores, are one of the features driving the increased Web site traffic. Such a function would no doubt please your retailers too.

Experiential Marketing

Experiential marketing, in which consumers come face to face with your new products and get to try them firsthand in an entertaining environment, is increasingly being used to break through the new product and media morass. Even simple techniques such as food product sampling have become far more sophisticated in recent years, moving beyond the grocery store aisle to the streets, sporting arenas, movies, and concerts. Psychomarketing is even entering the field. Companies are distributing products to consumers in vacation settings in the belief that this will produce a positive mental association between the

> **"Using guerrilla marketing** at the front end of a launch is a great way to create buzz. But the guerrilla marketing tactic has to make strategic sense. Many times, I see guerrilla marketing that doesn't tie back to the product. Your tactic has to reinforce the strategic message and set the stage for what's to come later in your launch campaign."
>
> — *Scott Russell, Chief Marketing Officer of MRA Group, Syracuse, New York, and Philadelphia, Pennsylvania*

product and having fun. The official term for this is "environment-conditioned marketing," a phrase coined by Market Connections International in Montclair, New Jersey.[5] Marketers of all kinds are hitting the highways and byways with their new products. They're even going onto the Internet, where customers can request specific product samples. The concept of mobile marketing vans, too, is getting more and more elaborate, with such programs as the Beneful Smart Spa, which Purina used to help launch its new Beneful dog food. The Smart Spa was set up in a number of cities, showing dog owners the latest trends in canine care and, of course, providing the new dog food for hungry pooches to taste test.

> **"A nontargeted approach** that casts the widest net possible for your media relations effort doesn't work. You have to be clear about who you're targeting and why. It's important to mount a concentrated effort. It's really relationship oriented; it's knowing what writers write about, and that takes listening and asking instead of just continually sending and waiting for their 'Please take me off your list' e-mail."
>
> — *Cori Barrett, Account Director for Access Communications, San Francisco, California*

A study by experiential marketing firm Jack Morton offers some food for thought about launch events designed to help consumers connect directly with a product: The firm's survey of 800 people found that experiential marketing is more effective with women than with men. Forty-three percent of women said experiential marketing is the medium most likely to cause them to purchase a product or service quickly, versus 29 percent of men. Among the Generation Y members of the survey group, 40 percent rated experiential marketing as the medium most likely to drive quick purchase response. The survey also asked people what they liked most about an experiential marketing event, and tops on the list — with a 61 percent response rate — was experiences that incorporate entertainment. An on-site representative who could talk to them about the product was also important to a large majority of those surveyed.[6]

Product Placement

When you start seeing stories about consumer giants like Procter & Gamble signing up to be represented by talent management agencies, it's time to officially proclaim that TV and movie product placement is a blistering hot marketing trend. There's even a new ad hoc think tank, the International Product Placement Research Council (IPPRC), being organized to research the practice; IPPRC comes complete with university researchers who hope to determine, among other things, the return on investment for product placements.

As Rich Frank, a Walt Disney television veteran who founded a brand-placement shop that was quickly gobbled up by the Firm, a Beverly Hills, California, talent-management company, told *The Wall Street Journal*, "If you were doing 'Friends' today, instead of a coffee shop, you'd have them gather in a Starbucks."[7]

Jumping on the product placement bandwagon can be expensive, but if you have a product with star power, like the MINI Cooper in the *Austin Powers* movie sequel, it might be the way to go. Clearly, the country's marketing giants see it as an effective way to break through the media clutter that is hampering more traditional launch techniques.

24

GENDER SPEAK: REACHING AMERICAN WOMEN

In a lengthy essay entitled "Women Roar: The New Economy's Hidden Imperative," management guru Tom Peters reported these statistics to show women's influence in the marketplace: "Women are responsible for 83 percent of all consumer purchases. Home furnishings ... 94 percent. Vacations ... 92 percent. Houses ... 91 percent. Consumer electronics ... 51 percent. Cars ... [women] make 60 percent of purchases, significantly influence 90 percent. Services the same story: choice of a new bank account by women ... 89 percent of the time. Health care ... 80 percent of decisions, over two-thirds of all healthcare spending."[1]

If that doesn't wake you up to the economic clout exerted by American women, consider this additional tidbit from Peters' essay: "Add up women's role as 'purchasing officers' for consumer products for their families and their significant role as professional purchasing officers for corporations and agencies, and, in effect, you have an American women's economy that accounts for over half of the U.S. GDP ... about $5 trillion."[2]

Even though, as Peters notes, American women constitute the largest economy on Earth, it wasn't until the past few years that marketers started to focus on whether they were doing a good job of reaching this most important audience. A spate of recent books, including Faith Popcorn's *EVEolution: The Eight Truths of Marketing to Women*, Mary Lou Quinlan's *Just Ask a Woman: Cracking the Code of What Women Want and How They Buy*, and Martha Barletta's *Marketing to Women: How to Understand, Reach, and Increase Your Share of the World's Largest Market Segment*, have helped close the knowledge gap about how to market effectively to women.

As trend guru Faith Popcorn and her firm's creative director, Lys Marigold, wrote in *USA Today Magazine*, "Besides the overwhelming economic reality, there is a second reason that EVEolutionary marketing [i.e., women-centric marketing] is so critically important in the marketplace. It's the biological one ... females process information differently because their brains are wired differently. They hear, acquire and use language in their own way, which accounts for the fact that girls generally speak earlier than boys, articulate their feelings more easily and see themselves more as links, not as loners."[3]

The field of gender-specific marketing is, in fact, relatively new, noted Barletta, who is president of The TrendSight Group, a Chicago, Illinois, area consultancy that helps Fortune 1000 companies attract more customers, investors, and management talent by improving their communications to women. "Marketing to women can be compared to where marketing to kids was 15 years ago," she said. "We know the target has money to spend, and we know they're different — but not too many people know how to put together a comprehensive program women will respond to."[4]

Here are more insights from Popcorn, Barletta, and other experts to consider when you want to fashion a launch plan that truly speaks to women:

- "Marketing to women is over. Marketing with them as partners is key to getting their dollars." That's the driving belief behind

> **"Get out and influence** the influencers. One of the things that Schiefflin did with their Dom Pérignon brand to ensure that restaurants keep it on their menu and to thank them for keeping it on the menu (at $45 per glass) is to have 'Flute Nights.' Schiefflin brand people visit really upscale bars and order Dom. Modeling behavior is really important for on-premise business, and selling high-end champagne is a visual endeavor. We show how to drink it, and others start ordering it."
>
> — *Fannie Young, Brand Manager for Schiefflin & Somerset, New York, New York*

Mary Lou Quinlan's book, *Just Ask a Woman*, which also happens to be the name of her New York City-based marketing firm. Quinlan, who formerly was chief executive of advertising giant N.W. Ayer & Partners, said that "marketing to women means thinking of them as a target to be sold or talked to. I believe in marketing with women, treating them as business partners, and listening to them throughout every step of the market process."[5]

• Word of mouth is all the rage, but according to Barletta, few discussions about the topic take into account the fact that "word of mouth is much more leverageable when marketing to women than to men. The simple act of talking to one another, sharing experiences and observations, is one of the fundamental bonding mechanisms of female gender culture."[6]

Barletta's advice: Make sure your initial stimulus for creating buzz is relevant to women.[7]

• "Put a smile on her face," suggested Quinlan. "Women need a laugh in their lives. They do respond to humor that makes sense for a particular brand. Not every brand is funny."[8] Quinlan also recommends thinking of "your customer as your sister, your mother, your best friend. She can detect a fake relationship in a second."[9]

• "Women believe people are the most interesting aspect of any situation," said Barletta. "Companies need more personality in their marketing."[10] That's why Popcorn advised connecting your female consumers to each other to connect them to the brand. "This is based on the fact that women love to share ideas, feelings, dreams, fears and most of all, information. They form spontaneous communities, whether it's at the playground, gym, or out in cyberspace ... [This is about] building and supporting a community of females — a healthy place where your brand is a prominent, helpful, active, fully contributing member."[11]

• Marina Maher, founder of Marina Maher Communications, a New York City PR firm known for its expertise in launching products for women, told us: "As marketers, we've grown from stereotypically aiming everything at men to marketing to a very feminine, independent individual today. In the early '80s, the trend was to reach women through the 'superwomen' strategy: 'I bring home the bacon, fry it up in a pan.' Today, we market to her mind, body, and soul — not to one part of her."

• Barletta pointed out that one generation of women can lead marketers to another generation of women. "Throughout the day, [women] seek to reinforce relationships by offering ideas to help with whatever aspect of life comes up in the conversation," said Barletta. "So even though 'women 35-plus' is not the target for a youth-oriented brand like the Ford Focus, each woman in this age group has daughters, sisters, nieces, and neighbors who are. The more women you reach with your message, the more you multiply the impact of your media budget."[12]

• To address the fact that women receive and evaluate information differently than men do, Popcorn suggested marketing to what she calls a woman's "peripheral vision." Women, she wrote, "have retractable antennae that scan everything — seeing and hearing the world on all levels, picking up clues, weaving together threads, intuiting, and inferring the inner meaning. Some might refer to this phenomenon as female observation. I have labeled it peripheral vision. That is where you want your product to appear — in a surround sound of opportunity found in the natural settings of her daily life."[13]

• Don't position a product or service that could be used by either sex as being for women only or the woman's version, advised Rebecca Maddox, a founder of Maddox Smye, LLC, a Naples, Florida-based consulting firm that trains companies to market and sell to women. She is also coauthor of *How to Get Rich Selling Cars to Women!* "The women you want most won't buy it if it's for women only," Maddox pointed out. "Instead, write the message so that it's clear you know who I am. I will respond to that, and you don't need to tell me it's for women. Also, if a product is for women only, men won't buy it, whereas if it is positioned as a product for men, women will buy it."

25

MAKING SENSE OF
THE MATURE MARKET

"**W**ill you still need me,** will you still feed me, when I'm sixty-four?" So sang The Beatles on their *Sgt. Pepper's Lonely Hearts Club Band* album in 1967. Try matching the image painted by that song's lyrics with the reality of Sir Paul McCartney's life today, when 64 is no longer decades away for the aging rocker. You'll quickly get an inkling of why marketing to people age 50 and up these days is so challenging. Far from losing his hair, digging weeds in the garden, and going for a ride on Sunday mornings, McCartney is married to a 30-something woman, still packing 'em in at rock concerts around the world, and lobbying for animal rights. In short, as *Brandweek* has pointed out, "he's the perfect poster boy for the aging generation [the Beatles] influenced in youth."[1]

McCartney exemplifies the fact that the generation now moving inexorably through middle age toward the so-called golden years is far, far different from previous generations. Yet in too many instances, marketers miss the mark when targeting mature consumers with new products because they still believe in the outdated image that Lennon and McCartney painted in "When I'm Sixty-Four." Even worse, many marketers avoid the mature market altogether, relying on myths that portray the mature adult population as a homogeneous band of nonspenders who can't be jolted out of their established brand loyalties and buying habits. But anyone who wants to cling to those outdated ideas will have to ignore these facts:

- Forty million Americans will enter the 50-plus age group during the next 20 years.[2] During the first decade of the 21st century, the 55-plus age group will increase in absolute terms by 21 percent, while the 18 to 44 population segment — ever the darling of marketers — will decline by 1 percent.[3]

- Consumers age 50-plus control 70 percent of total wealth and represent 50 percent of discretionary income in the United States.[4]

- According to the National Bureau of Economic Research's Consumer Expenditure Survey, consumers age 40 and older account for 64 percent of all expenditures on entertainment, 73 percent of all catalog sales, and 62 percent of purchases related to shelter.

- While households headed by persons age 40 to 64 represent 44 percent of all households, they spend 50 percent of all grocery store dollars.[5]

- Mature consumers spend their considerable discretionary income not just on themselves but also on others. Twenty-eight percent of toys and 26 percent of clothes for kids five and under are purchased by mature consumers who are buying them for grandchildren.[6]

- Many marketers continue to believe that discretionary income peaks when people are in their 50s, but per capita discretionary income actually doesn't peak until consumers hit their late 60s, and it doesn't decline much after that.[7]

Reaching the mature market requires understanding it. The first myth to erase from your memory is the notion that mature consumers are all the same. If we consider mature consumers to be anyone age 40 and over, there are at least four distinct market segments:

- Back-end boomers, the people born between 1955 and

1964, were too young to be influenced by the many defining moments that shaped older baby boomers. Some of them weren't even born when President John F. Kennedy was assassinated; they didn't protest the Vietnam War or go to Woodstock. In short, their life experience has differed considerably from what is typically described when people talk about the baby boomer generation.

• Front-end boomers, born between 1946 and 1954, are the real me-generation boomers, growing up in the years of economic expansion right after World War II. When people talk about all the stereotypes that go along with the baby boomer label, this is the group they're referring to. This generation came of age in the 1960s, with all that implies about their formative years. The leading edge of the group is now 58 years old. If you add in the folks born during World War II, you have a group of people aged roughly 50 to 62 that you could label as preretirees.

• People aged 62 to mid-70s, called active retirees, had childhoods that were shaped by the Great Depression and World War II. In the past, people in the older part of this group were considered to be well into their senior years, but improvements in life expectancy and health care mean this generation has changed. The last thing anyone in this group wants to be called is a senior citizen. While chronologically older, their emotional age is much younger.

• Today's true seniors are the 75-plus age group. Because the Great Depression and World War II were formative experiences for this generation, their values and attitudes were deeply affected by these seminal events. Yet even here, stereotypes can be way off base because many people in the younger part of this age group are definitely not ready for the rocking chair: Think of former Senator John Glenn returning to space at age 77.

Grasping the differences among these four distinct market segments is critical to developing a launch plan that succeeds in bringing mature consumers to your brand. Consider the challenge of reaching the group in this light: "A 50 year old is about as similar to a 75 year old as he is to a 25 year old."[8] Here are some other things to consider as you craft a plan to take advantage of the huge buying power of America's mature consumers:

- The stereotypical image of baby boomers emerged 30 years ago when front-end boomers were in their mid-20s. Not only is this image hopelessly out of date, but it also overlooks a significant sociological finding. "Sociologists tell us that as we age we become more unalike," according to Carol Morgan and Doran Levy, authors of *Marketing to the Mindset of Boomers and Their Elders.*[9] Any group of 55 year olds has had extremely diverse life experiences, yet marketers cling to the old notions that insist all baby boomers are the same.

  Breaking open this myth, as well as myths about the true senior generation, requires meeting and getting to know a wide variety of mature consumers. If your launch team is made up of people in their 20s and early 30s, as many teams are, make sure the real voice of the mature consumer is being heard. Bring target customers into your version of Idea Camp. This is a great way to ensure you're not just buying into the many stereotypes about how mature consumers behave. Ask them what beliefs they hold and how that will affect their response to your new product. Talk to them about the features and benefits they want in new products.

- Morgan and Levy also disputed the idea that getting mature consumers to switch brands is difficult. "The reality," they wrote, "is that those 40 and older are not distinguished by their brand loyalty."[10] One reason the myth continues to live on, Morgan and Levy pointed out, is that most mature households have only one or two people, so it takes them longer to use up products. Extending the time period over which consumption by brand is tracked provides evidence that mature consumers are actually no more brand loyal than younger consumers. This directly contradicts the notion that trying to lure mature consumers to your new product is a waste of resources. In addition, marketers need to recognize that baby boomers, who have been experimenters all their lives, are unlikely to stop trying new brands as they age.

• No one in any of the four mature market groups, not even those in the true senior segment, wants to be reminded he or she is getting older. Avoid using the word "senior" at all costs. "Marketing to seniors by implication, rather than spelling it out, might be the best way to go," according to Kurt Medina, president of Rose Valley, Pennsylvania-based Medina Associates, a direct response marketing firm specializing in the 50-plus market.[11]

Here's a good example of how to achieve success with this segment: Nestlé's Stouffer's brand recently ran a promotion targeting seniors for its frozen food line. Consumers earned free CDs for sending in box tops. The CDs were Frank Sinatra and Ella Fitzgerald recordings, so the promotion implied its target market without ever using the word "senior."[12]

• While some mature consumers — especially those who are retired and need to watch their budgets closely — aren't buying big-ticket items, they are willing to spend money on modest indulgences. In other words, they'll trade up in their small purchases. This is likely to become an even more predominant factor in the mature market as the baby boomers, who have been active consumers throughout their lives, move into their retirement years. Savvy marketers will focus their products and their launch messages to leverage this "indulgent" behavior.

• Great service is more important to the mature market than it is to other groups. "As people age, they tend to become more demanding in general because they've become more confident and know what they want," said Jan Chandler, managing director of Westport, Connecticut-based Greenfield Consulting Group.[13] Make sure you've covered all your bases when it comes to delivering service to support your newly launched product. Also, consider events or other consumer interactions that let you show the mature market how great your company's service can be. You'll win friends and customers!

• Don't assume that people's attitudes toward products alter dramatically as they age. "For instance, someone who wanted a fun, responsive car at 38 doesn't flip into a totally different mindset at 44," wrote Carol Morgan and Doran Levy. "Instead of touting zippy cars solely for those under 30 and stodgy cars with ample seats for the mature, cars can be positioned for a mindset that transcends age."[14]

• Do recognize the important changes that occur with aging. "As people get older, the way they process information changes and goes from the left brain — logical, linear, data-driven type of thinking — to the more right-brain approaches — intuitive, emotional, and holistic," according to John Migliaccio, Ph.D., past chairman of the American Society on Aging's Business Forum on Aging.[15] This and other knowledge that is emerging about the mental aspects of aging clearly has implications for those who are creating launch messages targeted to the mature market. Building a knowledge base of this information to share with all launch team members can have a tremendous impact on the success of your launch program.

26

CROSS-CULTURAL LAUNCHES:

SOLVING THE

HISPANIC MARKET RIDDLE

The rapidly increasing diversity of the American population discussed in Chapter 2 offers both opportunities and challenges for launch teams. Crafting a launch strategy that leverages the escalating buying power of the nation's growing ethnic groups can be a treacherous task if you've never tried it before.

Many companies are fairly new to ethnic marketing. The 2000 U.S. census pointed out the remarkable growth of the country's ethnic population, motivating numerous companies to jump into the cross-cultural marketing fray. Not everyone got it right the first go-round, offering further evidence of just how hard it can be to successfully launch a new product that's specifically targeted to an ethnic group, or to attract ethnic consumers to a new product made for the general market.

As the demographic data in Chapter 2 showed, the Hispanic population is outstripping the growth of all other groups in the United States. For this reason — as well as the fact that this is a particularly complex population to market to — we have provided specific tips to consider when launching products to Hispanics. Our goal here is to encourage you to think about the cross-cultural marketing challenge and, perhaps most importantly, to drive home the point that any company that overlooks the growing importance of America's ethnic diversity is turning its back on a huge opportunity to build market share.

Here are the most important things to consider when marketing to Hispanics. (Bear in mind, though, that many of these concepts apply to the Asian and African American markets as well, so think of them as food for thought for any cross-cultural launch program.)

- Hispanics come from different countries with different cultural practices, historical references, and political viewpoints. People whose roots lie in Cuba differ in many ways from those whose roots are in Mexico, for example. Dealing with this diversity is a huge challenge. (Needless to say, the same thing is true of the country's Asian population, which is made up of people from widely diverging cultures.) One size definitely will not fit all when it comes to marketing to Hispanics; after all, this is a group that tends to be called one name (Hispanics) east of the Mississippi and another name (Latinos) west of the Mississippi.

- One way to successfully navigate through this potential minefield of diversity is to work with local ethnic associations. They can provide valuable insights and information that will keep you on track when developing launch strategies and messages. Immerse yourself in the community and don't be afraid to ask questions. Better to ask up front than to make wrong assumptions and offend your target market through ignorance. Any time you're tempted to overlook this advice, just think back to the infamous instances in which companies chose product names that turned out to be embarrassing when translated into languages other than English.

- The complexity of the Hispanic population has implications for the type of media you'll use for your launch. While Hispanic print media are growing in number and in circulation, radio directed at Hispanics has struggled. "Radio is a very personal medium, and it is difficult to be personal with people with such different backgrounds," said Ricardo Brown, news director of Radio Unica, the first national, 24-hour Spanish language radio network in the United States. Speaking at the winter 2004 meeting of IPREX, a partnership of leading independent public relations firms, Brown said that there can be vast differences even within seemingly similar parts of the populations. "For example, a 50-year-old Cuban who has lived in Miami for 30 years is very different from a 20-year-old 'rafter' who arrived recently." There are important similarities across the group, however, that marketers should be aware of, Brown pointed out. These include:

• All Hispanics identify with success; it is the common goal and bond.

• Hispanics do not want to be talked down to; they represent a sophisticated market of people who characterize themselves as hard working, ambitious, risk taking, and proud.

• At the same IPREX gathering, Roberto Vizcon, news director of Telemundo 51 in south Florida, explained that one of the biggest challenges for his station — and similar stations across the country — is the enormous volume of news they have to cover. These stations broadcast not just U.S. national news and local market news but also general Hispanic information and major events in Hispanic countries around the world. To get through with information about a launch and pitches for the media to cover your introduction, Vizcon recommended using stories that empower Hispanics. He added that using spokespeople or talent who have lived the immigrant experience, which many Hispanics share, helps overcome cultural differences.

• As *Convenience Store News* reporter Jenny McTaggart wrote in October 2003, "There's also the risk of 'Hispanisizing' food products, which can actually devalue a brand in some consumers' eyes." Jennifer Woods, executive vice president of The San Jose Group, a Chicago, Illinois-based marketing firm, told McTaggart, "Many foreign-born Latinos, who make up well over half of the segment, come to the United States with the aspiration of eating [foods] 'Made in the USA.' While they may appreciate bilingual packaging on, say, breakfast cereal, it doesn't mean that they want a Hispanic version of a U.S. brand they already like."[1]

• In the same article, Chris Durren, a product manager with Austin, Minnesota-based Hormel Foods Corporation, recommended sharing information about Hispanic consumers with retailers. "Our retail customers are clamoring for this information, and we're right there to give it to them. We're helping them build the right sets for the right products at the right stores."[2]

• Much has been made of the brand loyalty of Hispanics. But like most things Hispanic, it's more complex than it looks on the surface. According to the 2002 Yankelovich/Cheskin Hispanic MONITOR study, "Store shelves are stocked with hundreds of brands and products that are not available in most Hispanic countries of origin. Not only are the products and brands new to many Hispanic consumers, but the labels are also written in English, making the purchase decision even more difficult. Thus, when 61 percent of Hispanics claim 'it's very difficult to get me to change brands once I find one I like' they are not necessarily saying they are brand-loyal as they are using the brand name they recognize to ensure they make a good purchase decision."[3] The implications for launch: Provide an easier purchase experience through better in-store information, Spanish translations on labels, and accurate depictions of product use to improve the odds of your new product inspiring brand loyalty from Hispanics.

• A survey conducted by the Association of Hispanic Advertising Agencies (AHAA) in 2003 dispelled the myth that young Hispanics prefer English and English-language media, and that only older Hispanics consume Spanish language media. "The AHAA surveyed 10,000 Hispanic households and discovered that 68 percent of young Hispanics are Spanish-dominant or bilingual," the Associated Press reported. "They also consume Spanish and English broadcast media at nearly equal rates, with Spanish-language television and radio outpacing English-language TV and radio." George L. San Jose, a Hispanic marketing pioneer who founded The San Jose Group in 1981, is also a big believer in using Spanish as the language of choice for Hispanic marketing. "People gravitate to their own language," he told a meeting of the Publicity Club of Chicago in 2003. "Use generic

Spanish; don't worry about capturing different Hispanic dialects. A good reference is Academia Real Espanol."[4]

• Consider direct marketing for your launch in this market. As reported at accutips.com, "Research has found that 70 percent of Hispanics do read their direct mail, and 35 percent want more," said Greg Bennett, president and creative director of Luna Bacardi Group/Aspen, a Culver City, California-based integrated marketing agency that focuses on the Hispanic market. In the same article, Jeff Bush, director of sales for Costa Mesa, California-based Specialized Direct Response, Inc., said, "One thing we've noticed is a higher response rate because these people are not invited as often [to participate in marketing offers]."[5]

• Another area in which Hispanics appear to be underserved — and one that has real potential for launching a new product — is Spanish language couponing. "Though Latinos are cost conscious, only 18 percent use coupons because of the language barrier," a national survey of Latinos showed.[6]

If you're starting to feel a little daunted by the challenge of reaching Hispanics in an effective way, here are some reasons to look on the positive side, compiled from articles in *Advertising Age*'s Multicultural Section in May 2002 by www.brandcentralstation.com:

• You'll have less competition in marketing to the Hispanic market (and other ethnic markets) because mainstream companies still have a long way to go in terms of volume. In some categories, you may have the field to yourself.

• A lot of culturally specific issues are covered only in ethnic media. So if you can leverage an issue of strong interest to Hispanics, again, you may have the field to yourself.

• Ethnic print media tend to be passed along with greater frequency than mainstream media, so you get more bang for your advertising or PR buck as many people read the same issue.

27

TODAY'S TEEN MOTTO:
HAVE MONEY — WILL SPEND

Early in 2004, Procter & Gamble began telling the world about Tremor, a marketing service it launched in 2001 that had already corralled 280,000 teens from age 13 to 19. Tremor's Internet site (www.tremor.com) recruits influential teens to help develop and promote product ideas and marketing programs that companies want to introduce and teens want to talk about. The teens are directly involved in the creation and launch of ideas and programs to build word of mouth among their peers.

Tremor, which planned to conduct roughly 20 campaigns in 2004, works not just with P&G's own brands but also with other brand-name companies in industries like entertainment, fashion, music, food, and

> "**You have to have** an intimate knowledge of the enemy. You need to know exactly what the category looks like and what each competitor's product stands for in that category. When you have an accurate picture of the competitive landscape, you can pinpoint where your product/brand fits."
>
> — *Marina Maher, Founder of Marina Maher Communications, New York, New York*

beauty. As *Forbes* magazine reported, this new approach to teen marketing "grows out of a profound dissatisfaction among advertisers with conventional media, particularly network TV ... Teens in particular are maddeningly difficult to reach and influence through advertising ... when they do catch TV commercials or print ads, these jaded consumers often ignore the marketing message."[1]

Sounds like a lot of work to go after the teen generation, doesn't it? But the group's demographics show why it's worth it. The U.S. population of teens aged 12 to 19 currently numbers nearly 33 million. If you include young people up to age 24, you have a market of 60 million people. Demographers eventually expect Generation Y, a.k.a. the Millennials, to eclipse the size of the baby boomer generation at its peak.

This group represents tremendous buying power. Teens spent an average of $103 per week in 2003, according to Teenage Research Unlimited (TRU), a Northbrook, Illinois, market research firm focusing on the teen market. Total teen spending for 2003 was $175 billion, up 3 percent from the previous year.[2] The TRU research indicates the teen market is more recession proof than the adult market. The data show that teens spent 5 percent more of their own money in 2003 compared with 2002, even though their parents didn't increase the amount of money they gave to teens over the same period. "Thanks to its unique circumstances — a great deal of disposable income paired with fewer recurring debts — the teen segment tends to have a much bolder attitude toward spending than does the general population," said TRU vice president Michael Wood.[3]

During the group's preteen and teen years, this rapidly growing population will establish brand preferences that will extend into their adult years. Sites like Tremor that focus on friendly chatter among peers to deliver targeted messages are the direction you'll need to take if your product is aimed at this major market segment. Here are several ideas on how to maximize both the buying power of teens and their brand loyalty, which increases as they move through their teen years.

- Reaching teens in a way that is not intrusive is critical to success, according to Samantha Skey, vice president of 360 Youth, the media and youth marketing arm of New York City-based Alloy, Inc., a media, direct marketing, and marketing services

company targeting Generation Y. "Teens are barraged with messages and don't want to be bothered by a brand that interrupts
their daily activities," Skey said. "Teens want to learn about
products in their own voice, from their friends or in a setting that
is comfortable. If you can get the peer-to-peer thing going, your
product can really catch fire."

• Teens like to discover things. They will "dig or diss" products.
And if they like a product, they will seed it with their friends.
That's why Tremor has been able to sign up nearly 1 percent of
the teen population to participate in its marketing campaigns.
Teens will fill out surveys on what they think about a product,
particularly if you offer them something in return.

• "Teens respond to companies that are giving back to the community," Skey said. "Lots of products are getting smarter about
aligning with causes because teens say that companies have a
responsibility to give back. If it's a meaningful cause that has
something actionable for teens and has a celebrity who is not
promoting a million other causes, it's a great model to employ."

• Make your campaign "real." "The Millennial generation has
a lot of trust issues," Skey pointed out, "so if you're a company
that is trying to build loyalty and you are disloyal, you will be
seen as evil corporate America. Young adults are smart and
see right through advertising, promotions, and marketing that
is not genuine."

• Launch campaigns directed at teens must be immediately
engaging and lifestyle relevant, according to TRU's Wood. Tie
in with what teens love and where they hang out.

• "To connect [with teens] in a meaningful way requires your
brand to learn about and live in the culture," said Mitch
McCasland, founder of Brand Inquiry Partners in Dallas,
Texas.[4] To many teens, that means the urban culture of hip-
hop and rap. He suggests that marketers immerse themselves
in this culture by reading such must-have references as *Hip
Hoptionary: The Dictionary of Hip Hop Terminology*, listening
to a local urban radio station or loading a selection of top

hits on an MP3 player, watching BET and MTV, going to the stores where teens buy their clothes and music, or even attending concerts.[5]

28

AVOID THE SAME OLD RUT

Everyone talks about thinking outside the box and doing things in a creative way, but every industry seems to have a formula for launch. We often attend elaborate briefings about opening new chain stores or introducing a new product from a major CPG company, all of which begin with, "Let's do this one differently." But what that usually means is, "Let's have a tiny twist to the formula we always use."

In these meetings, we hear things like "We always have a charity tie-in" or "We like to have a trade launch first at our booth and give out samples." Yes, certain marketing components should be part of almost every launch, but we find it interesting (and more than a little frustrating)

> **"People don't stick with the launch** long enough; they consider the launch done before they have actually launched. There's a first day on the shelf or an opening, and people think that's it. But that's the beginning, not the end. What you should do is use the start of the launch to fine-tune, see what worked, study how to bump this launch to get the maximum reward."
>
> — *Tom Bradley, Vice President and Director of PR for Mintz & Hoke, Avon, Connecticut*

that most companies define the launch for their agencies from the start, either by the size of the budget or by their own bias about what works and doesn't work in their industry. It appears to us that many marketing people are in a RUT.

Here's an example of how preconceptions about what works and what doesn't work can get in the way: We were launching a new candy geared to teens. The manufacturer was having a hard time selling it in to retailers, so the vice president of marketing asked us to develop a campaign geared toward kids age 12 to 18 that would reach them where they are in the summer. No problem. But when we asked if he had announced the new product to the trade press, he said, "No, that's a waste of money."

Now here's a case where the same old rut might have been a good thing! Retailers want to know you can generate a buzz, and the first way to show them that you can is by creating a buzz in their own trade publications. Companies should always announce a new product to the class of trade where it is going to be sold. Because candy is sold virtually everywhere these days, it was important for our client to alert trade publications that reach all categories of candy retailers, including drugstores, convenience stores, entertainment venues, mass retailers, groceries, and candy stores. In addition, with candy being sold in new venues such as home goods stores, office supply stores, and hardware stores, we needed to reach out to publications that cover those fields as well. And everyone, of course, has to get into business publications so the industry starts talking about the new product. Once you educate the retailers who can potentially sell your product, then you can begin telling consumers where to buy it.

Making What Already Works Better

How do you tell the difference between being in a launch rut and sticking to a launch approach because it really works for you? Also, how do you know if your biases about what works and what doesn't work in your product category are dictating what you choose to do? To answer these questions, you need to evaluate each component of your launch, a step that all too many companies skip in the rush to move on to the next launch coming down the pike. It's that merry-go-round problem again. By the time you're clear on the results of one launch, you're already well into the planning or even the execution of the next launch. Finding enough time to reflect is hard when the launch carousel never stops.

The solution: Build assessment and continuous improvement into the launch process. That means taking action all along the way to not only guarantee the current launch will be the best it can be, but to ensure that your launch team is also learning valuable lessons that will make its next launch even better.

The tool for doing this is called After Action Reviews (AARs), a technique many in the business world are adopting from the U.S. Army, which has been conducting AARs for decades. Marilyn Darling, president of the Boston, Massachusetts-based consulting firm Signet Consulting Group, has studied the army's AARs in depth and has also looked at how companies such as Harley-Davidson and Shell Oil have used the process to improve key parts of their businesses. As she explained it, an AAR differs significantly from the typical postmortem or retrospective review process that many people use at the end of a launch or other significant business event. "Instead of occurring only at the finish of a project, AARs occur throughout the life of a project," Darling said. "AARs are about looking forward; the whole purpose is to improve the next time around."

Key Differences between a Postmortem and 'Living Learning' Practices

A typical retrospective:

- "Learning" happens at the end of the project.
- Called for after failure or high stress.
- The meeting is planned after the project or event.
- One meeting with all participants in one room.
- Reviews the entire process.
- Produces a detailed report leading to recommendations.
- Focuses more on dissecting past performance.

A living AAR practice:

- Learning happens throughout the project.
- Planned for any project that is core to business goals.
- The meeting is planned before the project or event.
- Meetings with smaller, task-focused groups.
- Focuses on key issues relevant to going forward.
- Produces an action plan participants will implement.
- Focuses more on planning for future success.

© Copyright, Marilyn Darling, Signet Consulting Group

On the subject of using AARs to improve launches, Darling pointed out: "Every marketing plan is a hypothesis, particularly in a dynamic market. Things are happening in your marketplace that mean what used to work isn't working any longer. What system do you have in place that enables you to ask what will work now? That's what an AAR will help you achieve. It's part of building your thinking muscle; you're building the ability to fix problems."

Just as the army uses AARs in the field after every action, we recommend you use an AAR at every major step along your launch trajectory to gain iterative learning. For instance, if your launch includes a series of events at different venues or in different cities, instead of waiting until all the events are over to review what went well and what didn't, you would hold an AAR after each event. Then, you could use your new knowledge to make the next event even better. As Darling explained, "An AAR looks forward before it looks back; it's more about tomorrow's success than a postmortem of yesterday's failures."

Another key principle of the AAR process is that the review takes place at the organizational level where the work actually gets done. In other words, it's not the chiefs sitting around a table speculating on why their plans went awry — it's the worker bees who actually were engaged in the work, and who had the clearest view of the situations that resulted in success or failure. This process not only produces better learnings but also gives the team members "ownership" of their learnings. It's one thing to be told to do something different next time by a supervisor; it's another to be part of a meaningful discussion in which you decide what needs to change to make things better, based on the experience you just had.

AARs are not meant to be time consuming. Here's the simple process that Darling has witnessed many times in visits to the U.S. Army's Combat Training Centers. The group:

1. Reviews what the unit intended to accomplish (the overall mission and commander's intent)

2. Establishes the "ground truth" of what actually happened by means of a moment-by-moment replay of critical events

3. Explores what might have caused the results, focusing on one or a few key issues

4. Gives the unit the opportunity to reflect on what it should learn from this review, including what they did well that they want to sustain in future operations, and what they think they need to improve

5. Concludes with a preview of the next day's mission and issues that might arise.[1]

Note that determining what worked well is as important as figuring out where improvement is needed. Team members need to decide if the rut you're in is a well-established path that will lead to more success or whether you're just in the same old rut going nowhere. By using AARs, your launch team can significantly improve its chances of success for both current and future launches.

Bubbling up Ideas

One often-overlooked source of ideas to help you dig out of a launch rut is brand advocates throughout your own company. As the Energy Brands case in Chapter 21 showed, reaching beyond the launch team to involve everyone in the organization can provide just the spark needed to reignite a tired launch program. Tim Volk, president of Kelliher Samets Volk (KSV), a marketing firm with offices in Burlington, Vermont, and Boston, Massachusetts, called employees "the biggest beacons of a brand."

We're big believers in having an employee prelaunch event so everyone in the company hears about the new product before you go public with it. Not only is this a good practice for building an inclusive corporate culture, but it also helps prevent unfortunate situations that can occur when employees aren't informed about what's happening on the new product front.

For instance, journalists have told us how frustrating it is to attend trade shows and ask the booth staff about new products. Time after time, reporters find that the sales team can't answer questions about a new product because they haven't been briefed. Trade shows are great places to take advantage of media interest, but that requires preparation and having the information reporters want — and what reporters want most is to know what's new.

What you want to create is the situation that Sheryl O'Loughlin described at Clif Bar: "We have to be careful as we get bigger to make sure we include employees so everyone can play. We lose great insights when we don't include people internally. We go to events around the country, and when women talk to our people, they connect. We do not hire outside people to work our events; we feel they can't explain the emotion of the brand like we can. Our employees are masters. People connect, and the word spreads."

How do you build a culture that leads to employees who are strong brand supporters? Here are some additional ideas from Tim Volk, whose agency focuses on building brands from the inside out by making sure employees are involved in defining and supporting the brand:

- **SHARE THE BRAND THINKING WITH YOUR EMPLOYEES.** Too often, brand strategy development is an intellectual exercise among only the marketers and company leadership. After it's completed, the brand vision is then spread among the masses, customers and employees alike. That's bad. Employees should know the brand so they're well prepared to uphold the vision. Not including your employees in marketing changes can mean confusion, frustration, and breakdown.

- **GET HUMAN RESOURCES ON BOARD.** Your Human Resources department can help troubleshoot reality gaps and brainstorm ways to make your ideas work. You may be planning to enter the market with a message about how your phone reps are the most knowledgeable in the industry, but your HR manager might tell you there's work to be done in that area to uphold your claim. Having HR involved from the beginning can help you identify ways to include employees, who in turn will be more prepared to make your customers even happier.

- **EMPLOYEES ARE TARGET ONE.** Employees should be the first — and most important — target for a launch campaign. Employees will pay far more attention to a campaign's message than prospective customers will. Telling them first not only reinforces your brand promise and personality to this important audience (so they can deliver what you expect), but it has logistical value as well. If you're advertising a new offer that is going to send customers running to the phones, it's best to have employees familiar with the product that's inspiring all those push calls. Employees can also help point out any problems and last-minute details that need to be addressed before you roll out your campaign.

• **LISTEN.** Frontline employees see and hear more from customers in a day than some marketers do in a year of focus groups and surveys. Do you have systems in place to collect their valuable insights? Find a way to systematically gather and analyze customer feedback to employees. Your employees will feel valued, and your customers will see improvements before small issues become full-blown problems.

Step Off That Merry-go-round

If your company is doing a high volume of launches, it can be hard to step off the launch merry-go-round and try something new and different. When there's always a new launch coming before you've finished the one you're working on, it's easier to just rely on the tried and true methods you've always used. But heed this good advice from marketing author Seth Godin: "The safest thing you can do is to be risky. The riskiest thing you can do is to play it safe."

Here's an example of what can happen when a company and its creative agency decide not to play it safe. RUDS was a start-up manufacturer of men's compression shorts with a built-in testicle support system that renders jock straps unnecessary. With advertising too cost prohibitive for the small company, KSV created a targeted public relations campaign designed to generate multiple product reviews in geographic areas where RUDS had good distribution. Another campaign goal was getting attention for the company in the business press to help raise more capital.

Now, KSV and its client could have sent out an ordinary press kit. That would have been the safe route. Instead, they decided to push the envelope (literally) and sent media targets a black box, printed with intriguing and humorous copy, that contained two walnuts pushing out on the sides of the box. The exterior box copy featured names of high-profile college teams that used the RUDS product. The interior copy and walnuts offered a graphic and humorous explanation of the product's benefits.

The results: More than half of the reporters who received the box called the contact number before the KSV media follow-up team had a chance to place its own follow-up calls. Even more important, every reporter and editor at the sporting goods trades wrote articles about RUDS, generating an average of $5,000 per month in new business through the company's 800 number. And dozens of articles appeared in the consumer press, most of which carried the 800 number for ordering as well as names and locations of local stores.

The unusual boxes also helped generate trade leads. A mailing to 200 retail stores got a whopping 72 percent response rate from store managers. In addition, the press coverage helped build name recognition and credibility for RUDS. No wonder the campaign earned "Best of Show" honors at the Publicity Club of New England's Bell Ringer Awards program, which recognizes the most successful public relations campaigns from agencies all over New England.

This is just one of many examples we could offer that show the benefit of having fun with your launch. By not taking itself or its product too seriously, RUDS was able to achieve and exceed all its objectives.

We can easily imagine how another management team and another agency could have pushed this launch in the opposite direction with a serious approach stressing product benefits. We can also imagine the yawns that would have produced among media members.

If you're stuck in a launch rut, stop and consider how you could put the fun back into the process by taking a humorous approach to your next launch effort. Of course, there are many product categories where a serious approach is the only option. But there are also many, many product categories where humor can go a long way toward helping to make that all-important connection with media and consumers. Tickle a few funny bones. In short, lighten up!

Finally, we want to remind you of the age-old wisdom that cautions not to expect a different result if you continue to do the same old thing. Frankly, this is one area that really puzzles us about the whole field of launch. New product after new product meets a quick and untimely death, yet marketers continue to use the same launch processes and techniques. We urge everyone in marketing to consider adding new elements to launch, evaluating the effectiveness of these elements, and then accepting or rejecting them as part of the next launch. We also suggest studying different types of launches in industries outside your own. Looking beyond your industry for new techniques can yield fresh ideas that might work well in your category. Talking to new vendors and interviewing different types of vendors can give you lots of new ideas and ways to improve your existing methodologies.

Reach outside your comfort zone for your next launch. Get out and talk to new people. You won't learn anything by sitting in your office all day. When you walk around, chat with people, see how your business is being done in other parts of the country, find out what competitors are doing, and ask what companies in other fields are using for their launches. That's when you'll come up with the clever ideas that will help you avoid getting stuck in a launch rut.

29

TAKE HOME POINTS

We hope we've provided you with the salient trends, challenges, and advice you'll need to propel your future launches to success. While both the planning and implementation stages involve myriad details, in the end, it's the basics that provide the foundation for an effective new product launch. If you follow the *10 Proven Strategies* recapped below, you'll begin and end your launch journey on a path that others have already charted successfully.

We urge you to review this list each time you embark on a new launch and consider it your GPS (Global Positioning System). Just check your instruments, rev up those launch engines, and you're on your way!

Launch Strategy #1:
Treat Launch As a Separate Phase

If you think of the new product development process as a huge jigsaw puzzle, launch is an important piece of that puzzle. In Robert Cooper's Stage-Gate® Process, production and launch are coupled as the final stage of new product development. We believe launch should be its own stage because the elements that make up launch (or commercialization) are critical to a new product's success. Establishing a Launch Stage gives this process the attention it truly deserves. Advertising, public relations, promotions, special events, POS, guerilla marketing, e-commerce, and the Web are the engines that drive sales, and they deserve consideration long before the first package rolls off the assembly line.

You should begin thinking about launch the minute you decide to produce a new product. In today's highly competitive marketplace, the integrated marketing communications team can easily spend the same amount of time creating a launch as the product development team spends designing and manufacturing the product. Start early and give launch the planning and execution time it requires.

Launch Strategy #2:
Have a Plan

Carefully choreograph your launch so everything you do is part of a master plan. Be sure your launch team develops the plan together, so that all the elements mesh seamlessly. Timing is everything with launch, and we urge you to consider all the possible ways/times/methods you can use to introduce your product to its various target audiences.

Launch Strategy #3:
Don't Carve Your Plan in Stone

It's great to have a plan, but if you find one particular element of the campaign is performing head and shoulders above the others, then do more of that and less of something else. Being flexible is one of the keys to launch success.

Launch Strategy #4:
Learn to Live with the Inevitable Delays

No one ever thinks their launch will be delayed, but empirical evidence says 70 percent of launches are delayed at least once. On the flip side, sometimes a launch can be accelerated by a leak to the media or by a competitor's move in the market. Plan for the possibility that your launch will be delayed or accelerated. In addition, you might want to consider what you would do if a competitor interrupted your launch — by intention or by accident — with an announcement that derailed it. Plan for all possibilities that relate to timing, so you'll be prepared no matter what happens.

Launch Strategy #5:
Spend Money on Products That Are "New"

Spend your launch money on products that are really new and that will grab consumers' imagination. Because there are so many products being introduced each year, pick a new product from your lineup with media potential. Whenever possible, build your launch campaign around a product with sizzle. If the product fits into a new trend, if it has unique features never seen before, if it is new technology, if it makes life easier in a new way, then it's worthy of a major launch campaign. Be realistic: Not all new products are blockbusters. And no matter what agencies you select to help with your launch, if the product isn't really new and doesn't captivate consumers, it's going to be really hard to build the buzz necessary to meet your sales objectives. Be honest with yourself about how newsworthy your product or service really is before you embark on an expensive launch campaign that will yield marginal results. Finally, don't "sort of" launch a product and then ask an agency to launch it as if it's never been introduced before. (If you send out a press release announcing a new product, many editors consider that a launch!)

Launch Strategy #6:
Assemble an Expert Launch Crew

Make sure you have the right people on your launch team. Select talented agencies you enjoy working with and whose judgment you trust. Choose agencies because you like their style, their people, their track record, and because you feel confident they will push the envelope and encourage you to make the right creative decisions. You are going to spend a great deal of time together, and your working relationship is critical to success. Find partners who exhibit the right blend of strategy and implementation: Even the best strategy can bomb if it isn't implemented flawlessly. Select people who understand your business but who aren't stuck doing the same old thing. Passion counts for a lot, and you want to partner with people who are as passionate about your business — and your new product — as you are.

Share information with your agencies, and treat them as partners so they can provide maximum effectiveness. Be a full participant on the team. It's true you are the client, but your role is similar to that of an orchestra conductor. You have to lead your musicians to play the best music they can at every performance. And don't forget to read your e-mails, review the creative product and comment by the due date, return phone calls promptly, and generally be as attentive to the "administrivia" as you are to the big decisions. With launch, the devil is in the details, and meeting deadlines is top priority.

Launch Strategy #7:
Brand/Product Managers Make the Best Team Leaders

The best launch leaders are totally devoted to a new product's success. They have the time and inclination to squire the product from inception to launch without the distractions of countless competing responsibilities. While the president of the company may seem like a great person to lead a launch, his or her responsibilities on so many other fronts can be a distraction from the new product launch process. Brand managers, whose sole responsibility is to lead the launch, make the best leaders; their future depends on successful product introductions, so their focus remains steadfast throughout the launch process.

Launch Strategy # 8:
Bigger Budgets Fuel Success

Be sure you have all the tools you need to be successful. So many times, companies spend all their money on new product development and have little left to devote to the actual launch. Launching new products costs money. You'll need research that you're willing to share with the media on how and why you've developed the product. (The media love statistics and other types of hard data.) Having credible spokespeople, both company insiders and a third-party expert who can attest to the product's importance, is imperative. Also a must in most product categories is lining up consumers who've used the product and who are willing to talk about it.

The single biggest obstacle to new product success is underfunding your launch. In today's competitive marketplace, it always takes longer and costs more to launch a new product than you expect. Research your budget to be sure it's realistic, and plan for the unexpected.

Launch Lesson #9:
Consumer-focused Spending Prevents Crash Landings

Marketing direct-to-consumers is all the rage now, from sampling to guerilla marketing to "presence" opportunities at events. The old adage, "try before you buy," is the new consumer mantra. Best of all, finding ways to introduce your product through nonadvertising means can be an inexpensive and effective way to build trial and drive sales. These alternative distribution methods can be critical in building consumer demand. Remember, if customers fall in love with your product and ask for it at retail, it's hard for store buyers to ignore such requests. In fact, it's one of the few ways left to combat the high costs of slotting fees. Go directly to consumers and have them plead your case at retail.

Launch Strategy #10:
Don't Overlook PR

Never before has public relations been such a critical part of the launch mix. Placing stories in the media where your customers congregate is essential to building the awareness and credibility that are essential for a successful launch. Know your customers intimately so you can develop story lines for print, broadcast, and the Web that will attract their attention. Keep your media messages sharp and focused so the features, benefits, and attributes that differentiate your new product come across loud and clear. Develop both short- and long-term media relations strategies so your new product doesn't burst upon the media scene one day and then crash and burn the next. Leverage consumer trends as much as possible to sustain interest in your launch beyond the introductory period. Remember, the most effective launches use public relations to build the brand and sustain it over time.

Good Luck on Your Launch Journey!

We hope you've found *New Product Launch: 10 Proven Strategies* to be as interesting to read as we've found it to write. Based on how much information there is to know about the launch process, and how much it changes every day, we now understand why this topic hasn't been written about before.

We're eager to learn more about your successful or challenging launches, or tips you'd like to share. We invite you to write to us at jschneider@schneiderpr.com to help us in our commitment to provide ongoing information about launch. Through our efforts and yours, we hope that launch will one day have its own chronicled best practices, and that people will freely share what they've learned so we can all be more successful in our new product launches.

Getting your launch off to a great start helps ensure it will stay on track as the process progresses. This Launch Start-up Checklist is a tool Schneider & Associates uses to help make sure we cover all the bases as we initiate a launch program. While here it's written from the agency point of view, client-side companies can easily adapt it to keep everyone marching forward in the right direction.

Launch Start-up Checklist

✔	CLIENT TO AGENCY BACKGROUNDING PROCESS	RESPONSIBILITY
	Client interviews and hires agencies	
	Client compiles all background information to share with the agencies	
	Client delivers brand and marketing plans and background information	
	Client arranges individual briefing sessions with agencies	
	Client articulates reporting structure and approval process	
	Client relays expectations for the launch, sales goals, distribution plans and channels, budget for each discipline	
	Client reviews objectives and expectations with agencies	

✔	CLIENT TO AGENCY BACKGROUNDING PROCESS (cont.)	RESPONSIBILITY
	Client arranges background briefing for all agencies	
	• Introduce all members of the internal and external teams	
	• Explain the product in detail, from R&D to benefits	
	Client assigns launch planning process work to agencies:	
	• Develop primary research	
	• Participate in focus groups	
	• Execute literature search	
	• Speak with industry experts and analysts	
	• Conduct media audit, talk to editors about the category	
	• Compile competitive audit	
	• Review existing research and insights	
	• Read analyst reports	
	• Obtain samples of competitive products	
	• Visit stores to see competitive product placement (look at mockup of how this product will fit into category at retail)	
	• Interview key company executives about product	
✔	AGENCY BACKGROUNDING PROCESS	RESPONSIBILITY
	Research company background, product information	
	Review past research from client	
	Review past PR/Advertising/Web/Promotions initiatives and results	
	Conduct audits (as needed):	
	• Media audit	
	• Advertising audit	
	• Communications audit	
	• Research audit (client & secondary research)	
	• Competitive audit & landscape	
	• Client/Competitor Web site audit	
	• Issues audit	
	• Risk assessment audit	
	Interview/meet with all appropriate client contacts	
	• Ask what they wish to get out of the client/agency relationship.	
	• Ask what success looks like.	
	• Ask about client's past experience working with agencies (do's and don'ts)	
	• Download previous PR work and results	
	• Review previous PR files	
	• Ask about client's approval process.	
	o Materials approval and sign-off	

✔	AGENCY BACKGROUNDING PROCESS (cont.)	RESPONSIBILITY
	o Plan/budget changes and sign-off	
	• Find out key meetings to attend (trade shows, sales meetings, etc.)	
	o What is the agency's role?	
	• Determine how client communicates internally and how to get agency in the loop	
	Media meeting with client, account team	
	• Present agency's media philosophy	
	• Present media audit results	
	• Complete media strategy worksheet	
	Share information among agencies	
	Discuss timing for launch (what if we are late, what if we are early? What if competitor tries to preempt our launch?)	
	Discuss crisis planning (what can go wrong, how would we deal with it?)	
✔	SYSTEMS/PROCEDURES DEVELOPMENT	RESPONSIBILITY
	Organize finances	
	• Create budget for launch	
	• Determine monthly projections for launch budget	
	• Set staffing model to meet budget	
	o Identify time frames when extra help will be needed	
	o Identify team downtimes and busy times	
	• Work out any budget sharing with other agencies	
	Filing – develop framework for both computer and central filing system	
	Subscriptions – Order subscriptions to any relevant trade, vertical, or consumer publications that we don't already receive (using purchase orders)	
✔	PROGRAM DEVELOPMENT/IMPLEMENTATION	RESPONSIBILITY
	Work with lead agency to conduct Idea Camp	
	Develop mission statement for Idea Camp	
	Host Idea Camp	
	• Determine theme for campaign	
	• Establish program elements	
	Divide responsibilities by agency	
	Research concepts and budgets	
	Meet with client to review top-line concepts from Idea Camp	
	Client/agencies agree on direction for campaign	
	Agencies finalize campaigns and budgets and present to client	

✔	PROGRAM DEVELOPMENT/IMPLEMENTATION (cont.)	RESPONSIBILITY
	Client agrees to campaign and budgets	
	Finalize goals, objectives, and strategies	
	Develop plan/program	
	• Determine what product(s) to include (i.e., media monitoring, message development, media training, crisis preparedness, etc.)	
	Create time line/workflow of deliverables	
	Create program measurement criteria and vehicles	
	Plan meeting to present program in person	
	Edit, revise, finalize program	
	Agencies execute campaigns	
	Build Web site to launch concurrently with PR campaign	
	Launch public relations campaign before advertising	
	Promotional campaign begins	
	Advertising begins	
	On-line advertising begins	
✔	EXTERNAL COMMUNICATIONS	RESPONSIBILITY
	Preferred method of updates and communication	
	• Determine whether client prefers phone calls, e-mail, paper	
	• Determine frequency/style of media monitoring updates (daily/weekly; e-mail/fax)	
	• Review other specific requests, e.g. preference for weekly activity updates, weekly conference calls, etc.	
	Billing	
	• Inform client what to expect on bills	
	o Agree on format (by project or a fixed fee)	
	o Inform clients that monthly activity reports, spreadsheets will accompany each bill	
	• Determine expense backup needs	
	• Alert client to prebilling of certain expenses	
	• Determine when client sign-off required for changes in budget, incremental expenses	
	• Determine direct expense spending levels that require client's prior approval	
✔	INTERNAL COMMUNICATION	RESPONSIBILITY
	Assign responsibility for internal monthly reports	
	Monitoring/Scanning	
	• Set up media scanning responsibilities	
	o Consumer publications	
	o Trade journals	
	o Factiva News Search (Dow Jones Interactive)	

✔	INTERNAL COMMUNICATION (cont.)	RESPONSIBILITY
	o LexisNexis	
	o eWatch	
	o NewsIQ	
	o General scanning/clipping service	
	• Create format for reporting ongoing monitoring to client	
	Set up To Do List	
	Set regularly scheduled team meetings	
	• Include other practice reps as appropriate; other agencies	
✔	MEASUREMENT/TRACKING/MERCHANDISING	RESPONSIBILITY
	Determine methods for tracking, measuring results	
	Secure clipping service, if necessary	
	Develop communication tools to keep client apprised of results	
	• Monthly/quarterly meetings	
	• Clip reports	
	• Memo merchandisers	
	• Printed merchandisers	
	• Video clips	
	Determine complete list of client contacts that should receive results merchandising	
	Track and update editorial calendars	
	Set up/maintain placement grid	
	Present client final measurement tracking materials	

INTRODUCTION

1. Figures for numbers of new products launched each year come from the Marketing Intelligence Service Ltd./Productscan® Online database of new products at www.productscan.com.

2. Ad budgets are according to Nielsen Media Research.

CHAPTER 1

1. Penn, Catherine, "2004 New Product Development Survey," *Stagnito's New Products Magazine*, February 2004, p. 24.

2. "How Can I Make My Line Extensions More Incremental," *Facts, Figures, & the Future*, October 13, 2003.

CHAPTER 2

Authors' note: Except where noted, all demographic data is from the U.S. Census Bureau.

1. Humphreys, Jeffrey M., "The Multicultural Economy 2003: America's Minority Buying Power," *Georgia Business and Economic Conditions*, Second Quarter 2003, Volume 63, number 2, pp. 2-6.

2. Tilove, Jonathan, "The Nation Evolves As Population Shifts," *The Sunday Republican*, March 21, 2004, p. I1.

3. Tilove, Jonathan, "Through Immigration and Exodus: A New Melting Pot," The Republican, March 22, 2004, p. E2.

4. Tilove, Jonathan, "America Moves to the New Sun Belt," The Republican, March 23, 2004, p. E4.

5. Tilove, Jonathan, "Heartland: Half Full or Half Empty," *The Republican*, March 24, 2004, p. E5.

6. Ibid., p. E7.

7. Tilove, Jonathan, "The Nation Evolves As Population Shifts," *The Sunday Republican*, March 21, 2004, p. I6.

8. "Over 60 and Overlooked," The Economist, August 8, 2002.

CHAPTER 3

1. Press release at www.yankelovich.com.

2. Elliott, Stuart, "Hunting for the Next Cool in Advertising," *The New York Times*, December 2, 2003, p. C19.

3. Ibid.

4. Press release at www.yankelovich.com.

5. "How Many Days Are Enough," *Facts, Figures, & the Future*, September 8, 2003, http://www.factsfiguresfuture.com.

6. Ibid., Elliott, Stuart.

7. Press release at www.yankelovich.com.

CHAPTER 4

1. *Plunkett's Entertainment & Media Industry Almanac*, 2002, Plunkett Research, Ltd., p. 17.

2. Berry, Jon, and Keller, Ed, *The Influentials*, The Free Press, 2003, p. 43.

3. Schiesel, Seth, "Can Cable Fast-Forward Past TiVo?" *The New York Times*, October 20, 2003, Section C, p. 1.

4. "Half of Internet Users Have TV, PC in the Same Room," *DIRECT Newsline*, September 17, 2003.

5. Elliott, Stuart, "Blacks Prefer TV Fare with Black Casts, but Tastes of Blacks and Whites Are Converging, Study Says," *The New York Times*, April 21, 2003, Section C, p. 12.

6. Ibid., Berry and Keller, p. 11.

7. Ahrens, Frank and Williams, Krissah, "Spanish-Language Media Expand," *Newsbytes*, Post-Newsweek Business Information, Inc., August 11, 2003.

8. Poza, Ins, "Pledge of Allegiance: Advertisers Can Shatter the Myth of Latino Brand Loyalty," *Adweek*, June 24, 2002.

9. Press release from Media Economics Group, January 13, 2004.

10. Ibid., Berry and Keller, p. 11.

11. Press release from Nielsen//NetRatings, March 18, 2004.

12. "Linking Online Media to Offline Sales," *Facts, Figures, & the Future*, December 2003.

13. www.pewinternet.org.

14. Nielsen//NetRatings press release, March 18, 2004.

15. Hindman, Matthew, and Cukier, Kenneth Neil, "More News, Less Diversity," *The New York Times*, June 2, 2003, Section A, p. 17.

CHAPTER 5

1. "Wal-Mart Update: Supersizing the Supermarket," *Times & Trends*, Information Resources, Inc., October 2003, p. 8.

2. "How Many Days Are Enough?" *Facts, Figures, & the Future*, September 8, 2003.

3. Ibid.

4. Beirne, Mike, "Future of Marketing," *Brandweek*, February 2, 2004, p. 28.

5. Tedeschi, Bob, "E-Commerce Report: Reporting Healthy Increase in Sales, This Holiday Shopping Season Was the Best Ever for Internet Retailers," *The New York Times*, December 29, 2003, online edition.

6. "ACNielsen Research Finds U.S. Sales of Private Label Consumer Packaged Goods Growing Much Faster Than Branded Products," press release from ACNielsen, September 18, 2003.

7. Pyle, Robert N., Statement Before the Federal Trade Commission Slotting Fees Hearing, November 8, 1995, www.ftc.gov/op/globa/slot.htm.

8. Wieffering, Eric, "Product-visibility Fees Are Hurting Consumers, Some Companies Say," *Star Tribune*, Minneapolis, March 7, 2003, p. 1A.

9. Food Marketing Institute's Web site: www.fmi.org/facts_figs.

10. Ibid.

11. "Slotting Allowances in the Supermarket Industry," www.fmi.org/media/bg/slottingfees2002.pdf.

12. Ibid., Eric Wieffering.

13. "Slotting Allowances in the Retail Grocery Industry: Selected Case Studies in Five Product Categories," Federal Trade Commission Staff Study, November 2003, p. vii.

14. "Channel Blurring: Driven By Consumer Changes," *Facts, Figures, & the Future*, June 9, 2003.

CHAPTER 8

1. This figure is according to the Pew Internet & American Life Project.

CHAPTER 9

1. Nelson, Emily, "Toilet-Paper War Heats Up With New, Wet Roll," *The Wall Street Journal*, January 17, 2001, p. B1.
2. Nelson, Emily, "Is Wet TP All Dried Up? — How One Toilet Paper Product Wiped Out After Its Launch," *The Wall Street Journal*, April 15, 2002, p. B1.
3. Ibid.
4. Frank, John, "What's Cooking in Food PR: The Scale of Food Launches Might Be Waning," *PR Week*, May 14, 2001, p. 19.
5. "Heinz Unveils New Blue Ketchup," *USA Today*, April 7, 2003, online version.

CHAPTER 10

1. Barboza, David, "Versatility Helps Oreo Fill Gaps in Market," *The New York Times*, October 4, 2003.
2. Sebell, Mark, and Yocum, Jeanne, *Ban the Humorous Bazooka [and Avoid Roadblocks and Speed Bumps along the Innovation Highway]*, Dearborn Financial Publishing, Inc., 2001, pp. 22-23.

CHAPTER 12

1. Only 70 executives out of the total 91 who completed surveys answered the question about total budget, so the figures in this section represent a smaller sample than the sample used in other chapters.
2. Keller, Ed, and Berry, Jon, *The Influentials*, The Free Press, 2003, p. 5.

CHAPTER 13

1. Griffin, Abbie, "PDMA Research on New Product Development Practices: Updating Trends and Benchmarking Best Practices," *Journal of Product Innovation Management*, Vol. 14, p. 440.

CHAPTER 15

1. Collins, Jim, *Good to Great*, Harper Business, 2001, p. 41.
2. Ibid., p. 177.

CHAPTER 17

1. Ries, Al, and Ries, Laura, *The Fall of Advertising & the Rise of PR*, Harper Business, 2002, pp. 241-243

CHAPTER 20

1. Bedbury, Scott, *A New Brand World*, Penguin Books, 2003, pp. 93-94.

CHAPTER 22

1. "Consumer Resistance to Marketing Reaches All-Time High, Marketing Productivity Plummets, According to Yankelovich Study," press release from Yankelovich Partners, April 15, 2004.

2. Nail, Jim, "Uncooking the Goose," Forrester Research and Intelliseek, December 2003.

3. Quoted from "Women Roar: The New Economy's Hidden Imperative," by Tom Peters, Tom Peters Company Press, 2001, p. 16.

4. Silverstein, Michael J., and Fiske, Neil, *Trading Up: The New American Luxury*, Penguin Group, 2003, p. 36.

5. Beam, Alex, "Gibson's 'Passion' for Movie Profits," Boston Globe, February 26, 2004, p. D1.

CHAPTER 23

1. Cyrot, Jean-Luc, Urdl, Christian, and Alves, Ignacio Garcia, "Networks Work: Viral Marketing as a Tool for Launching Innovations," *Prism*, 2003.

2. Beirne, Mike, "Future of Marketing," *Brandweek*, February 2, 2004, p. 32.

3 Bertolino, Keri, "Blogs: The New PR Medium?" *The Bell Ringer*, April 2004, p. 3.

4. Tedeschi, Bob, "Consumer Product Companies Use Web Sites to Strengthen Ties with Customers," *The New York Times*, August 28, 2003.

5. Wells, Melanie, "In Search of the Buy Button: What Makes Some Products Irresistible? Neuroscientists Are Racing to Find the Answer to That Question," *Forbes Global*, September 1, 2003, p. 34.

6. Shuler, Laura, "Experiential Marketing Survey," www.jack-morton.com.

7. Smith, Ethan, and Vranica, Suzanne, "Faces and Products Firms to Merge," *The Wall Street Journal*, March 19, 2004.

CHAPTER 24

1. Peters, Tom, "Women Roar: The New Economy's Hidden Imperative," Tom Peters Company Press, 2001, p. 20.

2. Ibid., Peters, Tom, p. 20.

3. Popcorn, Faith, and Marigold, Lys, "The Secrets of Marketing to Women," *USA Today Magazine*, November 2000, www.findarticles.com.

4. Barletta, Martha, "Pretty Maids All in a Row: How to Translate Gender-Specific Insights Into Impactful Tactics," *All About Women Consumers*, 2002, p. 2.

5. Raine, George, "What Women Want; Ad Agency Vet Helps Marketers Discern Female Buying Habits," *San Francisco Chronicle*, July 25, 2003.

6. Ibid., Barletta, Martha, p. 3.

7. Ibid., Barletta, Martha, p. 3.

8. Reyes, Sonia, "Girl Power Strategies: Do's and Don'ts," *Brandweek*, April 22, 2002.

9. Ibid., Raine, George.

10. Thatcher, Geoff, "Marti Barletta Teaches 'How to' Market to Women," March 17, 2003, People & Places That Rock Blog.

11. Ibid., Popcorn, Faith, and Marigold, Lys.

12. Ibid., Barletta, Martha, p. 3.

13. Ibid., Popcorn, Faith, and Marigold, Lys.

CHAPTER 25

1. Ebenkamp, Becky, "When They're 64," *Brandweek*, October 7, 2002.

2. U.S. Census Bureau.

3. Peters, Tom, "Women Roar: The New Economy's Hidden Imperative," Tom Peters Company Press, 2001, p. 24.

4. "Moving Beyond Age to Market Directly - and Appropriately to the Growing Mature Marketplace," www.accutips.com.

5. Morgan, Carol M., and Levy, Doran J., "Why Marketers Fail to Understand the Mature Market," *Quirk's Marketing Research Review*, December 2002, www.quirks.com.

6. Kinsman, Matt, "Forever Young," *Promo*, October 1, 2003.

7. Ibid.

8. Huberty, Tim, "Keep It Simple, Sonny: Thoughts on Conducting Focus Groups with Older Consumers," *Quirk's Marketing Research Review*, December 2001, www.quirks.com.

9. Ibid., Morgan, Carol M., and Levy, Doran J.

10. Ibid., Morgan, Carol M., and Levy, Doran J.

11. Ibid., Kinsman, Matt.

12. Ibid., Kinsman, Matt.

13. Ibid., Ebenkamp, Becky.

14. Ibid., Morgan, Carol M., and Levy, Doran J.

15. "Moving Beyond Age to Market Directly - and Appropriately to the Growing Mature Marketplace," www.accutips.com.

CHAPTER 26

1. McTaggart, Jenny, "Ethnic Evolution: The Hispanic Aisle Continues to Progress as Manufacturers Target the Country's Largest Minority Group," *Convenience Store News*, October 12, 2003.

2. Ibid.

3. "2002 Yankelovich/Cheskin Hispanic MONITOR Launched," November 12, 2002, press release, www.yankelovich.com.

4. Gorak, Katie, "Hispanic Audiences Present Thriving Opportunities for PR Professionals," October 8, 2003, www.publicity.org/monthlyoct03.htm.

5. "Targeting the Multicultural Marketplace: Filling the Direct Marketing Gap," www.accutips.com.

6. Guy, Sandra, "Latino Food Firm Looks to Benefit from Growing Market," *Chicago Sun-Times*, April 30, 2003, p. 69.

CHAPTER 27

1. Wells, Melanie, "Kid Nabbing: How P&G, Coke and Sony Use Teens to Push Products in Homes and Schools," *Forbes*, February 2, 2004, p. 84.

2. "Teens Spent $175 Billion in 2003," January 9, 2004, press release on www.teenresearch.com.

3. Ibid.

4. McCasland, Mitch, "Teen Marketing? Fo' Shizzle Dizzle," February 10, 2004, www.marketingprofs.com.

5. Ibid.

CHAPTER 28

1. Darling, Marilyn, and Parry, Charles, "After-Action Reviews: Linking Reflection and Planning in a Learning Process," *Reflections*, Volume 3, Number 2.

CHAPTER 1

1. Gillette Venus Razor printed with permission from Gillette

CHAPTER 3

1. *Trading Up* cover printed with permission from Michael Silverstein

CHAPTER 11

1. Subway logo printed with permission from Subway®

CHAPTER 12

1. $20 bill image printed with permission from The Department of the Treasury Bureau of Engraving and Printing

2. *The Fall of Advertising and the Rise of PR* cover printed with permission from Al Ries

CHAPTER 18

1. NECCO logo printed with permission from New England Confectionery Company

2. Hood Peak Treasures logo printed with permission from HP Hood

CHAPTER 20

1. *Free Prize Inside The Next Big Marketing Idea* cover printed with permission from Seth Godin

2. Old Mother Hubbard logo printed with permission from Old Mother Hubbard

CHAPTER 21

1. Luna Bar printed with permission from Clif Bar Inc.

2. Glaceau Vitamin Water printed with permission from Energy Brands Inc.

CHAPTER 22

1. Honey Dew Donuts logo printed with permission from Honey Dew Donuts